Ben Walsh

Empires and Citizens

Book 1

Contents

The Roman Empire in two pages!

753 BC Foundation of Rome

Period 1: The foundation of Rome to the conquest of Italy (753 BC to 270 BC)
At the start of this period Rome was just a collection of villages. By 270 BC the Romans had defeated many enemies and controlled all of Italy.

509 BC Rome got rid of Etruscan kings and became a Republic

LONG LIVE THE REPUBLIC

270 BC Romans conquered Italy (after many wars)

Period 2: The growth of the Empire (about 270 BC to about AD 200)
In this period Roman conquests continued steadily. Rome stopped being a Republic and officially became an Empire in 27 BC. By AD 117 the Empire reached its peak, and lasted another 350 years.

Hail Augustus!

44 BC Caesar Augustus became the first Roman emperor

AD 117 Roman Empire reached its greatest extent under Emperor Trajan

AD 122 Hadrian's Wall started

AD 212 All people living in Roman Empire (except slaves) became full Roman citizens

AD 253 Barbarians raided Roman Gaul

AD 313 Emperor Constantine made Roman Empire Christian

Period 3: The decline of the Roman Empire (about AD 250 to AD 476)
From the 200s onwards, Rome faced a range of problems. There were disputes and civil wars within the Empire. There were also problems running such a huge empire and defending it from invaders. Very gradually, the Empire declined. Eventually it collapsed and was divided between barbarian leaders.

AD 395 Empire divided into Western and Eastern Empires

AD 455 Rome sacked by barbarian invaders (Vandals)

AD 476 Last Roman emperor removed

Timeline markings: 800 BC, 700 BC, 600 BC, 500 BC, 400 BC, 300 BC, 200 BC, 100 BC, 1 BC/AD 1, AD 100, AD 200, AD 300, AD 400, AD 500

AD
Barbarian
BC
Christian
Citizen
Civil rights
Civil war
Conquer
Conquest
Emperor
Empire
Etruscans
Gaul
Republic
Ruler
Society
Vandals

The Roman Empire – a big picture

You may already have studied Roman Britain at Key Stage 2, but this does not mean you should not have another look. This unit looks at the Romans in Britain but also at the rest of the Roman Empire as well. The Roman Empire was huge and lasted for a long period of time – about 1200 years! But we can make sense of the Roman Empire by looking at three main periods: 753 BC to 270 BC, 270 BC to AD 200 and AD 250 to AD 476. Look at the timeline on the opposite page.

The citizens of the Roman Empire

We will also look at people in the Empire. The Roman Empire was a very large and complex society. There were free citizens with full civil rights and also millions of slaves with no civil rights. Rich and powerful Romans had more privileges than the poor. On the other hand, the Empire was democratic in some ways. You could rise through the ranks of Roman society even if you were not a Roman. Over 30 of Rome's 84 emperors were not born in Italy.

The importance of the Roman Empire

As it spread, the Roman Empire had a huge impact on the lives of people in Europe, North Africa and parts of Asia. The Romans brought their language, laws, religious beliefs, armies, buildings, food, wine and a whole lot more to all these places. We will look at the impact of the Romans on the rulers, citizens and slaves who all became part of the Roman Empire at different times.

Brain work

1 Read through these pages. Find at least four points or facts (more if you can) and put them in a diagram like the one below. We have done one for you.

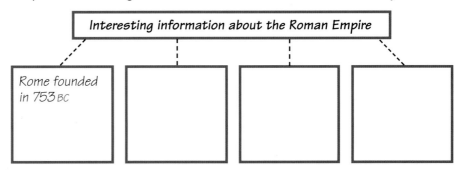

Interesting information about the Roman Empire

Rome founded in 753 BC

2 If you have studied the Romans before, think really hard to see if you can remember any extra points you can add to your diagram.

3 If you have not studied the Romans before, try to come up with some good historical questions about the Roman Empire that you would like answered. See if anyone in your class knows the answers.

OVERVIEW

The history of Rome is important because almost every modern society in Europe and America has based its laws and government on Roman ideas, and quite a few other societies have as well.

What's so interesting about the Romans?

When you first studied the Romans you may not have seen how their amazing achievements are relevant to your life today. If you look around carefully you might, like Phil in the cartoon above, be surprised how Roman ideas still influence our lives today.

Take buildings in Washington, for example. Many of the important buildings like the Capitol Building, where the USA's politicians meet, and the American Supreme Court, where important criminal cases are heard, look like they were built by the Romans hundreds of years ago. Phil concluded that Roman buildings were so magnificent that people have copied them ever since. Look at Sources 1–4 and see if you agree.

SOURCE 1a–b ▶

Reconstructions of Ancient Rome. Rome was built on seven hills. The most important hill was the Capitoline.
1a Rome seen from the River Tiber (the Capitoline Hill would be on the right).
1b The Forum (main business area) of Rome with the Capitoline Hill rising in the background.

SOURCE 2 ▶

The Roman amphitheatre at Arles in southern France. Amphitheatres were sports stadiums.

SOURCE 3 ▶

The American Supreme Court in Washington DC. This building and all the other American government buildings are in an area called the Capitol. This is named after the Capitoline Hill, which was the most important hill in Ancient Rome.

SOURCE 4 ▶

St George's Hall in Liverpool. This was built in the 1830s as a place for exhibitions and public meetings.

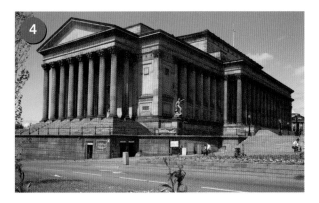

KEY WORDS

Amphitheatre
Archaeological
Aqueduct
Christianity
Forum
Government
Latin
Mosaic

1 Look at the drawings in Source 1. Do any of these buildings remind you of places or topics you have studied in history before?

2 Look carefully at Sources 1–4. Make a list of any similarities you can find between the buildings in Source 1 and the buildings in Sources 2–4.

3 Do any buildings in your home town look like the buildings in Sources 1–4?

4 Phil thinks that 'Roman buildings were so magnificent that people have copied them ever since.' Are you convinced?

SOURCE 5 ◄

Local council building in Victoria Square, Birmingham, built in the middle of the 1800s. The Victorians admired the Romans and built their most important buildings in the style of Roman buildings.

SOURCE 6 ▼

This is a mosaic showing a Roman chariot racer with one of his horses. The colours of his clothing show that he has been sponsored by a wealthy Roman, just like companies sponsor football teams today!

Phil has done a lot of research on the Romans. The more he researched, the more things he found that he thought were really impressive.

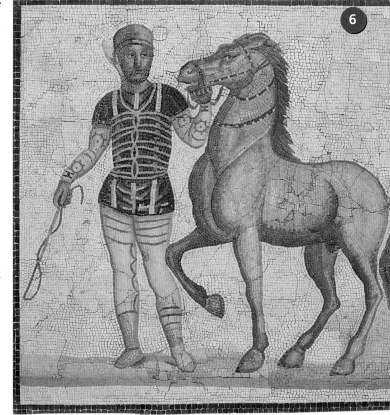

- One of the biggest things the Romans left us was their language. The Roman language was Latin. Some words we use regularly today, like exit, stadium and capital, are actually Latin words.

- The Romans were brilliant engineers. We can still see the remains of their magnificent roads, bridges, aqueducts and sewers. Many of London's sewers are still based on the original Roman layout!

- Roman government was effective and fair (you will find out more on pages 28–29). Many modern systems of government use Roman ideas today.

- The Romans had a very advanced legal system. Many countries today use Roman ideas, such as magistrates and rights of appeal, in their legal system.

- Rome became Christian in AD 313. This helped to spread Christianity all over Europe. This is one of the reasons why many people in Europe and America are Christian today.

- The Romans knew how to have fun. They had all-seater stadiums for their sports and they even had sponsors for the kits!

SOURCE 7 ▶

*An extract from a university
textbook called* A History of Rome,
published in 2001.

❛ At the end of the twentieth century several European countries still bear the imprint of Rome, though their people do not always realise it. The people speak a language based on Latin. The layout of their towns is 2000 years old. Their daily life, their holidays and even their names bear the stamp of Roman Christianity. Their art, literature and philosophy were often inspired by the Roman Empire. Their values (liberty, justice, law, honour, courage) are also 20 centuries old. ❜

7

So, I think we should all study the Romans. Their ideas still have a big influence on our lives today and we should know all about them.

Brain work

1 Your task is to help Phil explain why we should study the Romans. Collect four or five examples (more if you can) of ways in which the Romans influence the world today. Make a large copy of this table to help you gather and think through your ideas.

Aspects of Roman history which still influence us today	Examples

2 Use your examples to produce a talk to persuade your classmates that it is important to study the Romans because they influence our lives today. You could use ICT to create a slide show to go with your talk.

OVERVIEW

Rome started off as a small collection of villages in 753 BC. Its power grew through the Mediterranean and then across Europe and Asia to become an enormous empire. It reached its peak in about AD 120.

Rome conquers Italy

The Romans had their own stories about the origins of Rome. One story said that Rome was founded by the hero Aeneas. Aeneas was the son of the goddess Venus. Another story said Rome was founded by Romulus. Some versions of the story said that Romulus and Remus were the sons of Mars, the god of war. Romulus and his twin brother Remus were brought up by a she-wolf. When they grew up, Romulus killed his brother in an argument. Romulus then gathered the scattered farmers in the hills and valleys around the River Tiber. These people accepted Romulus as their leader. Romulus built a city for his people and called it Rome. He was the first king of Rome.

Not surprisingly, most historians do not believe either of these stories. The story of Aeneas was written in around 19 BC by the poet Virgil. This was over 700 years after the city was founded! Nobody knows how old the story of Romulus and Remus is. Romans probably did not know the origins of their city or their empire. However, in Virgil's time Rome was a great empire. To many Romans, it made sense that they were great because their city was founded by heroes who were related to the gods. Most historians think that Rome's development went something like the events set out in Source 2.

SOURCE 1 ▼
A bronze statue showing the she-wolf feeding Romulus and Remus. This would have been on display in one of the temples in Rome.

1

1 Which of the following ideas do you think is most likely to be true?
   a The Romans really believed the stories of Aeneas and Romulus.
   b The Romans liked the stories of Romulus and Aeneas because they were more exciting and entertaining than the real origins of Rome.

2 Do we sometimes change historical stories to make them more entertaining today, for example in movies?

3 Do you think the historians' explanation for the growth of Rome is more believable than the stories of Aeneas or Romulus? Explain your answer.

4 Look at the information in Source 2. Using the dates there, draw a timeline to show the conquest of Italy.

KEY WORDS

Greeks
Historian
Latins
Samnites
Senate
SPQR

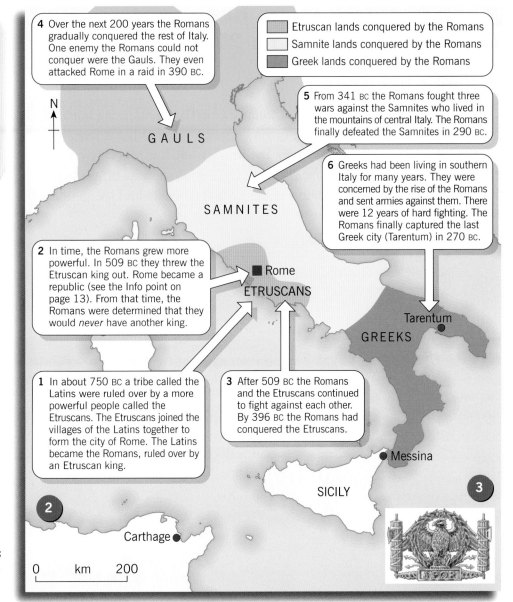

4 Over the next 200 years the Romans gradually conquered the rest of Italy. One enemy the Romans could not conquer were the Gauls. They even attacked Rome in a raid in 390 BC.

Etruscan lands conquered by the Romans
Samnite lands conquered by the Romans
Greek lands conquered by the Romans

5 From 341 BC the Romans fought three wars against the Samnites who lived in the mountains of central Italy. The Romans finally defeated the Samnites in 290 BC.

6 Greeks had been living in southern Italy for many years. They were concerned by the rise of the Romans and sent armies against them. There were 12 years of hard fighting. The Romans finally captured the last Greek city (Tarentum) in 270 BC.

2 In time, the Romans grew more powerful. In 509 BC they threw the Etruscan king out. Rome became a republic (see the Info point on page 13). From that time, the Romans were determined that they would *never* have another king.

1 In about 750 BC a tribe called the Latins were ruled over by a more powerful people called the Etruscans. The Etruscans joined the villages of the Latins together to form the city of Rome. The Latins became the Romans, ruled over by an Etruscan king.

3 After 509 BC the Romans and the Etruscans continued to fight against each other. By 396 BC the Romans had conquered the Etruscans.

N

GAULS

SAMNITES

Rome
ETRUSCANS

Tarentum
GREEKS

Messina

SICILY

Carthage

0   km   200

SOURCE 2 ▶
The Roman conquest of Italy.

SOURCE 3 ▶
The banner carried by the armies of the Republic of Rome. SPQR is an abbreviation. It means 'Senate and people of Rome'.

Brain work

Imagine the Romans had newspapers like we have today. Write a series of headlines which might have appeared in the period 750 BC to 270 BC. You should think about:

- the events a newspaper for Roman readers would choose to headline.
- the type of newspaper you are writing for (for example, a more serious paper like *The Times*, or a tabloid newspaper like the *Sun*).
- the length of your headline (usually only four or five words).
- your focus (for example, emphasising the Roman victories or emphasising the enemies' defeats).
- whether you will miss out any events on purpose.

Keep your headlines in a safe place – they will help you in the next few pages.

How did Augustus become the first Roman emperor in 27 BC?

Republic to empire

As Source 1 shows, the Republic of Rome carried on conquering lands after it had conquered Italy. It is pretty obvious from Source 1 that Rome conquered a great empire. However, the Romans did not officially call their conquered lands an empire. From 264 BC to 27 BC Rome was officially the Republic of Rome. The Republic was ruled by the Senate and the people of Rome (see the Info point opposite).

> **KEY WORDS**
> Carthage
> Legion
> Naval
> Senate
> Taxes

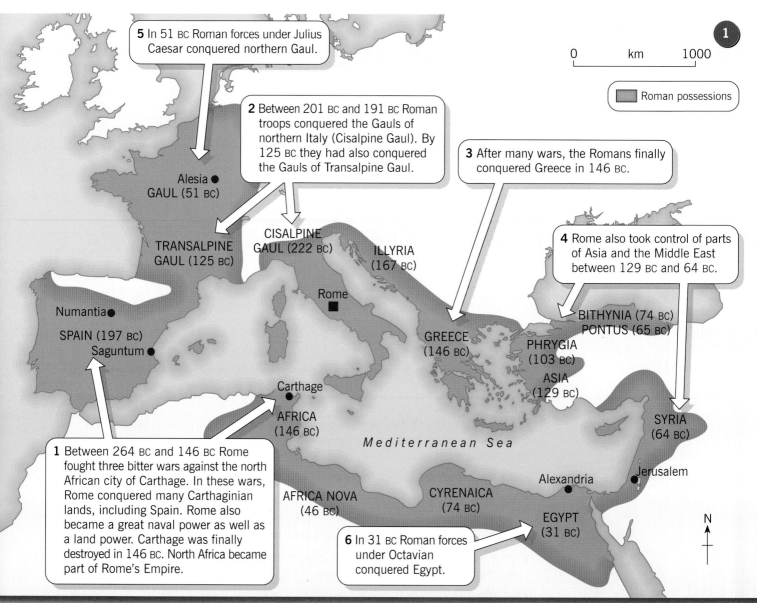

5 In 51 BC Roman forces under Julius Caesar conquered northern Gaul.

2 Between 201 BC and 191 BC Roman troops conquered the Gauls of northern Italy (Cisalpine Gaul). By 125 BC they had also conquered the Gauls of Transalpine Gaul.

3 After many wars, the Romans finally conquered Greece in 146 BC.

4 Rome also took control of parts of Asia and the Middle East between 129 BC and 64 BC.

1 Between 264 BC and 146 BC Rome fought three bitter wars against the north African city of Carthage. In these wars, Rome conquered many Carthaginian lands, including Spain. Rome also became a great naval power as well as a land power. Carthage was finally destroyed in 146 BC. North Africa became part of Rome's Empire.

6 In 31 BC Roman forces under Octavian conquered Egypt.

0   km   1000

☐ Roman possessions

1

Alesia ●
GAUL (51 BC)

TRANSALPINE GAUL (125 BC)

CISALPINE GAUL (222 BC)

ILLYRIA (167 BC)

Rome ■

Numantia ●
SPAIN (197 BC)
Saguntum ●

Carthage ●
AFRICA (146 BC)

GREECE (146 BC)

PHRYGIA (103 BC)

ASIA (129 BC)

BITHYNIA (74 BC)
PONTUS (65 BC)

SYRIA (64 BC)

Mediterranean Sea

AFRICA NOVA (46 BC)

CYRENAICA (74 BC)

Alexandria ●

Jerusalem ●

EGYPT (31 BC)

N ↑

Look back at the timeline you made for question 4 on page 10. Add the main events in Source 1 to your timeline.

Info point

How the Republic worked

- Senate: *A council of men from important and wealthy families. Places in the Senate were usually handed down from father to son.*
- Magistrates: *Officials chosen by the Senate who looked after the law, taxes, trade, etc.*
- Consuls: *Chief magistrates who dealt with the most important issues, especially Rome's many wars. Consuls were elected for a year so they did not get too powerful.*
- Tribunes: *These were important officials who presented the views of ordinary Romans to the Senate.*

SOURCE 1 ◄

The growth of Rome's empire up to 27 BC.

SOURCE 2 ►

A statue of a prisoner with his hands tied behind his back. The statue dates from the first century BC.

SOURCE 3 ►

A wall carving showing members of the Senate discussing an important issue.

By 27 BC, this had changed. In that year Rome officially became an empire and the first emperor took power. There were long-term and short-term reasons for this change. Here are the long-term reasons:

- As Rome conquered more lands, many Romans became unhappy with the rule of the Senate. Many Senators were corrupt. They had given themselves good jobs running Rome's new territories. They got rich from Rome's wars. At the same time, ordinary Romans just seemed to get higher taxes to pay for the wars.
- By about 100 BC the army was very large. In fact, there were several armies based in different parts of the Empire. The commanders of the army gradually became more important and more powerful than the Senate.

These developments eventually combined with other factors to cause the end of the Republic. Turn over to find out how.

Brain work

1 Look back at the newspaper headlines you created for the Brain work activity on page 11. Add some more newspaper headlines for the events on these two pages.

2 Add some subheadings to your headlines to give more details of the events. Look at a copy of today's newspaper to get an idea of how newspapers do this.

SOURCE 4 ◀

A statue of the Roman military commander Julius Caesar.

SOURCE 5 ◀

A statue of Octavian. Octavian was Caesar's great nephew, but Caesar adopted him as his own son.

The story of how the Republic became the Empire centres on two key figures, Caesar and Octavian.

Hail Caesar!

Julius Caesar was a brilliant military leader. He conquered new territories for Rome in northern Gaul. Caesar was also ambitious. In 49 BC he decided to take control of Rome. Between 49 BC and 45 BC he defeated rival army commanders who tried to stop him. He took control of Rome in 45 BC. Most Roman people supported Caesar because they were fed up with the Senate.

Caesar did not get rid of the Senate but he made himself dictator. This gave him more power than the Senate or the consuls. He introduced a range of measures to improve life in Rome. However, he was only in power for one year. In 44 BC he was murdered by Gaius Cassius and Marcus Brutus and other members of the Senate. His killers thought Caesar was planning to make himself king.

Caesar's death led to civil war between his supporters and opponents. Eventually, Caesar's friend Mark Antony and Caesar's adopted son Octavian defeated Cassius and Brutus. Unfortunately, Mark Antony and Octavian then fell out. Octavian finally defeated Mark Anthony in a great sea battle at Actium in Greece in 31BC.

Octavian was now the most powerful man in Rome. He controlled an army of 60 legions (about 300,000 men). That meant he controlled Rome. Like Caesar, he did not get rid of the Senate. However, there was no doubt about who ruled Rome. In 27 BC he became the Emperor Augustus, a title which meant 'majesty'. Rome was now officially an empire and no longer a republic.

Augustus turned out to be an effective and well-respected emperor. He ended Rome's wars and disbanded half of the legions. He concentrated on developing the security and trade of the Empire and its people. When Augustus died in AD14, the Roman Empire was strong and stable. But would it last?

KEY WORDS

Military

Rival

Tomb

1 Who supported Julius Caesar and why?

2 Why do you think Caesar was murdered?

3 Describe the stages which resulted in Octavian taking power in Rome.

4 What kept Octavian in power?

❝ After I had extinguished civil wars, and when I was, by universal consent, in control of everything, I was given the name Augustus by the Senate. The doorposts of my house were decorated with laurel. A crown was attached above my door. A golden shield was given to me by the Senate and Roman people with an inscription praising my courage, mercy, justice and piety. After that time I surpassed everyone in authority, but I treated my colleagues as equals. ❞

6

SOURCE 6 ◄

An extract from the list of achievements of Augustus, which was written on his tomb after he had died. There were 35 other sections like this on the inscription.

5 Read Source 6. Does this source prove that Augustus was a great emperor?

6 Look at Source 7. Does this memorial suggest that Augustus was a great emperor?

7 The memorial in Source 7 was built by Augustus himself. Does this affect your view of the memorial as evidence about Augustus?

SOURCE 7 ▼
A memorial to Augustus in Rome, built during his lifetime.

Brain work

In the Brain work activities on pages 11 and 13 you wrote some newspaper headlines. Now your task is to write a complete article for a newspaper front page. The news event you are reporting on is Octavian becoming Augustus – the first Roman emperor. Your article will need:

- a headline
- subheadings (your previous headlines should be useful here)
- an 'angle' – do you approve or disapprove of Augustus becoming emperor?

You also need to decide what information will be included in your article. You could mention all or some of these points:

- the actions of Julius Caesar.
- how and why Augustus became emperor.
- why the Senate became less important.
- why the army became more important.
- what kind of empire Augustus now rules.
- how Rome got this empire.

Aim for a word limit of 150 words. If you need to write more, ask your teacher first.

You could use a word processing or desktop publishing programme to create your article. Think carefully about how to set out your article. Below is a suggested layout, but you may have better ideas.

THE ROMAN NEWS

Octavian becomes Emperor Augustus

Emperor triumphs at Actium

New emperor pays tribute to Julius Caesar

What is keeping Augustus in power?

The Roman Empire at its height: Why was Trajan such a successful emperor?

We are going to fast-forward about 100 years from the death of Augustus. The Empire lasted well after Augustus. In fact, it continued to grow. We are now going to look at the Roman Empire in AD 117. Rome was reaching its peak, under the rule of the Emperor Trajan.

SOURCE 1 ▼
The Roman Empire under Trajan. Like most emperors, Trajan rose to power because he was a successful soldier.

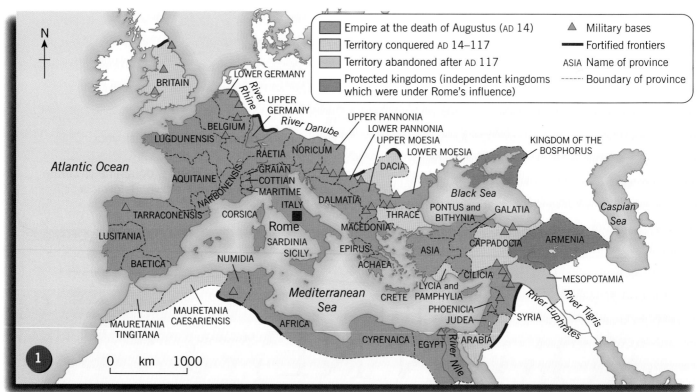

The city of Rome at the time of the Emperor Trajan was stunning. Sources 2 and 3a and 3b give you an idea of what it was like. The Forum was the central part of the city, where business and shopping took place. Rome had five different forums by Trajan's time. However, Trajan's was the biggest and the most impressive. The total area of Trajan's Forum was about the same size as 20 football pitches. It contained shops, libraries and statues. It was also beautifully decorated.

From documents written at the time we know that Romans liked to come to the Forum. It is worth remembering that most Romans lived in cramped blocks of flats on the outer edges of the city. Romans could walk around the Forum and admire the decoration and the statues. They would also meet their friends, talk, and go and have a drink. Great writers and thinkers used the libraries. Tourists used to love Trajan's Rome as well. The biggest attraction was the 120-metre high Trajan's Column. Read on to find out more about Trajan.

KEY WORDS

Administration
Arabia
Archaeologist
Archer
Auxiliary
Benefactor
Campaign
Cavalry
Dacia
Governor
Harmony

SOURCE 2 ▲

Trajan's Forum as it looks today. Only Trajan's Column is left standing. The buildings behind the column were built long after the Roman period.

SOURCE 3a–b ▶

Reconstruction drawings of the new Forum built by Trajan in AD 113. These drawings are based on the reconstruction which was created by historians and archaeologists at the University of California.

3a

3b

KEY WORDS

Legionary
Merchant
Mesopotamia
Province
Reconstruction
Tolerant

1 What do Sources 1–3 tell you about:
   a the wealth of the Roman Empire at its height?
   b what it was like to live in Rome?

2 How would seeing the Forum affect a visitor to Rome in the time of Trajan?

3 Source 3a–b shows two reconstructions of the Forum. Do you think they are accurate? Explain what information helped you to decide.

Long after his death, Trajan was remembered as the best Roman emperor. When later emperors were appointed, supporters used to wish that the new emperor would be 'more fortunate than Augustus and as great a ruler as Trajan'. What made Trajan so great?

Trajan's rule

There is a lot of evidence to suggest that Trajan was well respected. Although he was an emperor, he seemed to be able to talk to ordinary people and get on well with them. He was a soldier with a lot of military experience. This meant he had the loyalty and respect of the army. He treated the Senate with respect, although he was prepared to ignore their advice on important issues if he disagreed with them.

Trajan also had loyal support from the Roman provinces. He appointed many new Senators, most of them from the provinces of the Empire. He also appointed officials who were loyal to him to run the provinces. Trajan respected the religions and cultures of the provinces he conquered. The Roman Empire was generally tolerant and respectful towards other religions.

 The Emperor was chosen by the gods and acted in harmony with them. He listened to the advice of wise men in the Senate and devoted his life to fulfilling his duties. He was a father and benefactor to his subjects. He led free men and not slaves. And his friends as well as the nobility participated in the administration of the state. (4)

SOURCE 4 ◄
This is what a governor called Pliny thought of the Emperor Trajan. Pliny was appointed by Trajan. They wrote many letters to each other.

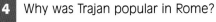

4   Why was Trajan popular in Rome?
5   Why was Trajan popular in the provinces of the Empire?
6   Read Source 4. What do you think of Pliny's views?

The wealth of the Empire

Trajan was able to make use of the enormous wealth of the Empire. Taxes flowed in from all the provinces. He also taxed wealthy Romans, but not as much as he taxed the provinces. Officials who wanted to pass on their jobs to members of their family had to give more than 5 per cent of their pay in tax. Trajan also forced all Senators to invest one third of their wealth in land or businesses in Italy. This helped to solve the problem of unemployment, which troubled Italy in Trajan's reign.

Trajan also brought enormous wealth into the Empire from his conquests in Dacia (see Source 9 on page 23). Above all, Trajan was able to raise money by taxing the growing trade within the Empire.

Trajan spent this wealth wisely. A lot of it went to pay for the army. However, a lot of it went on buildings like the Forum (see Sources 3a–b on page 19). He also built aqueducts which supplied water for the city.

SOURCE 5 ▶
A merchant ship in a Roman port.

(see Sources 3a–b on page 19).

Info point

Roman trade

The Empire was criss-crossed with trade routes which ran along the Roman roads and by sea. Some of the main trading areas were:

- Gaul: *gold, silver, iron, glass, marble, pottery, linen.*
- Greece: *marble and other building materials, wine, linen, pottery.*
- Spain: *gold, silver, iron, copper, lead, horses, marble, wine, wheat, barley.*
- Britain: *lead, tin, iron, copper, wool, hides.*
- Egypt: *grains, glass, drugs, papyrus, wild animals.*
- Dacia: *gold, salt, horses, timber.*

As well as the provinces, merchants in the Empire also traded with India, Arabia and East Africa.

SOURCE 6 ▶
A wall decoration from Trajan's time showing how successful farming was. Meat was in great demand in Rome at this time. This is evidence that Romans were prosperous because meat was expensive. Romans must have had money to spare.

7   What made the Roman Empire wealthy?

8   Is Source 5 useful for historians looking at how successful Roman trade was?

9   What use is Source 6 to historians?

The Roman army

Of course, we cannot forget the army. The Roman army was the most powerful army in the world. All Roman emperors depended on the army. Trajan was no exception. He was a soldier before he became emperor.

The Roman army was very large. There were usually 30 legions and a large number of auxiliaries – about 350,000 men in total. It was divided into armies which were stationed around the Empire (see Source 1 on page 18).

It was a full-time army. This meant Roman legionaries were well trained. They also served for at least 20 years so they were highly experienced. Legionaries could march long distances and fight ferociously.

Legionaries were also skilled builders. Wherever they went they built forts, roads and bridges. This meant that supplies could always get through to them.

The army was well equipped. Legionaries all had armour, weapons and equipment like digging tools. Just as important, the legions had their own cooks, doctors and even clerks in charge of pay.

Auxiliary units usually provided cavalry, archers or any other type of support the legions needed.

Legionaries were all Roman citizens. They were selected for their loyalty to Rome. They also got a share in any loot the army won in its campaigns.

The army had an extensive system of forts and military bases. They used torches and smoking beacons to warn other forts if there was trouble. The excellent Roman roads meant that Trajan could bring together large numbers of troops very quickly to deal with any problems.

The army was also a great advertisement for the Roman way of life. Most conquered peoples were impressed by the legions, their forts and their roads. Many people made a living supplying the legions with food, clothes, etc.

10 Draw your own version of the diagram above, but try to reduce the amount of writing. For example, you could simply write 'Large army of 30 legions' for the first point. Thinking like this helps you to remember important information.

11 Look at Sources 7–10.
   a Which sources support points made about the army in the diagram?
   b Do the sources raise any points not mentioned in the diagram?
   c Add a quote or a piece of information from Source 10 to your diagram.

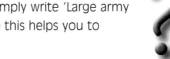

SOURCE 7 ▶

Roman legionaries building a fort (top) and a pontoon bridge (bottom) during one of Trajan's campaigns.

SOURCE 8 ▶

Roman legionaries in battle.

SOURCE 9 ▶

The leaders of the Dacians surrender to Trajan after losing to him in battle in AD 107. Trajan forced the Dacians to pay gold, silver, works of art, fine foods and other luxuries to Rome.

SOURCE 10 ▶

The Greek writer Polybius describes the Roman army. Polybius was writing some time before Trajan's rule, but the processes he describes were still used in Trajan's times.

❝ **If it ever happens that a large body of men break and run in battle, the tribune calls the legion on parade and brings to the front those who are guilty of leaving the ranks. He then reprimands them sharply, and finally chooses by lot one tenth of the men who have shown themselves guilty of cowardice. Those who draw the lot are then mercilessly clubbed to death. The danger of drawing the lot threatens each man equally. The Romans find this is the best possible way to repair any weakening of their warlike spirit.** ❞

Brain work

Imagine you have left school and are travelling across Europe. You have reached Rome but have run out of money! However, you have just got a job as a tour guide in the city. Your job is to take people around Trajan's Forum and up to the top of Trajan's Column (there is a staircase inside).
Look back at pages 18 to 23. *Either*:

1 Prepare notes so that you can talk to people looking around the Forum, *or*
2 Prepare a guide book so that people can look around the Forum and Column themselves.

You will need to decide what to say about:

• the buildings in the Forum and what the Romans did there.
• what the Forum looks like now and how different it was in Trajan's time.
• what Trajan was like as a ruler.
• where the money came from to build it all.
• why the Roman army features so strongly on Trajan's Column.

You may already have studied Hadrian's Wall at Key Stage 2. You could add some more points to your tour notes or guide book about Hadrian. He was the next emperor after Trajan.

OVERVIEW

The Roman Empire was enormous. So how did the emperor control it? The army certainly played a big role. However, for most citizens of the Roman Empire, it was simply better to be part of it than not part of it.

KEY WORDS

Freedman
Mithras
Pax Romana
Persia
Reaping
Villa

Pax Romana in pictures

For much of the period from Augustus (27 BC) to about AD 250 the Roman Empire was stable and peaceful in most of its provinces for most of the time. This peace and stability was called Pax Romana (which is Latin meaning 'Roman Peace'). But how was this Pax Romana achieved? The simple answer is that we are not sure. Most of the documents, buildings, objects and so on from Pax Romana are long gone. The ones that do survive are our sources. Archaeologists and historians have to interpret the sources available the best way they can to try to understand Pax Romana.

SOURCE 1 ◄
A wall carving showing a Roman reaping machine.

SOURCE 2 ►
A reconstruction drawing of a typical British dwelling before the Roman occupation of Britain. There were also larger settlements called hill forts.

SOURCE 3 ►
A reconstruction drawing of a legionary fort at Wallsend on Hadrian's Wall. Note the settlement that has grown up near the fort to supply the needs of the soldiers.

SOURCE 4 ►
A reconstruction drawing of a Roman villa. Wealthy villas like this would have had their own bath houses as well.

SOURCE 5 ►
A modern reconstruction drawing of the Roman town of Trier (in Germany) in winter.

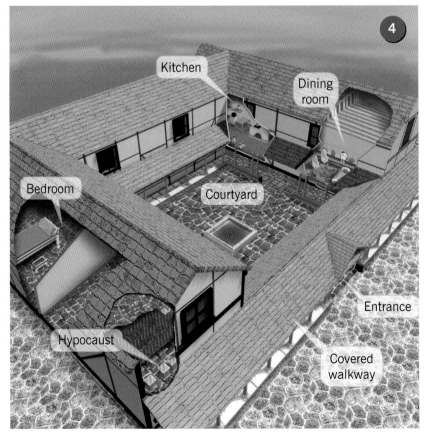

SOURCE 6 ◀

A wall painting from around AD 200 showing the god Mithras. He is shown sacrificing a bull. This was the traditional sacrifice to Mithras.

SOURCE 7 ▲

The tombstone of Anicius Ingenuus. Anicius was a doctor with the army stationed on Hadrian's Wall. He was the son of a Greek freedman (a slave who had been set free). He died some time in the early AD 200s.

SOURCE 8 ◀

A wall painting showing lawyers arguing a case in court.

SOURCE 9 ◀

A reconstruction drawing of a street of shops in a Roman town.

SOURCE 10 ▶

A reconstruction drawing of the Roman baths of Caracalla in Rome. These baths were some of the most magnificent in the whole Empire. The baths were a key part of Roman town life.

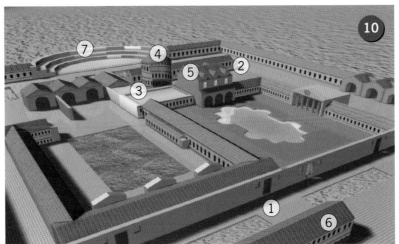

1 Entrance

2 Toilets

3 Tepidarium – lukewarm room

4 Caldarium – hot room filled with steam

5 Frigidarium – cold bath

6 Refreshments

7 Entertainment area

Brain work

Work in pairs or small groups and examine Sources 1–10. Use the sources to come up with possible reasons why the Roman Empire was stable and prosperous for most of the time. Historians call this 'hypothesising'. You need to:

- look at each source (look at the details in each source and also the text with it).
- consider how each source helps to explain the peace and stability of Pax Romana. For example, you might think that Source 1 explains Pax Romana because it suggests Romans were never short of food, so they were happy.
- consider how strongly your ideas are supported by each source or by other sources as well.

You could use a table like the one below. Source 1 has been done for you to give you an idea of how you might work.

Source	This source suggests that...	I think this because...	This helps to explain Pax Romana because...
1	Romans produced a lot of food.	It shows they had to use machines to collect all the food they grew.	People in the Empire were never short of food, so they were happy.
2			
3			
4			
5			
6			
7			
8			
9			
10			

Extension work

Look back at your table and look at column 2. Decide whether you think the word 'suggests' is right for each source. Possible alternatives might be:

- definitely shows that...
- strongly suggests that...
- may possibly indicate that...

Pax Romana in words

Roman citizenship

One key factor which held the Empire together was Roman citizenship. Most people wanted to be citizens of Rome because this position brought privileges. One privilege was army service. Although risky, army service could bring glory, a job for life and a good pension. Citizens also paid lower taxes. Above all, being a citizen of Rome brought status. In AD 212 Roman citizenship was given to all people in the Empire except slaves. The result was that an Italian, a Spaniard, a North African or a Briton could all feel that they were 'Romans'.

A multicultural empire

The Roman Empire did not try to force everybody to be like the Romans.

* The Romans borrowed ideas from other people (like armour from the Gauls or art from the Greeks).
* The Romans generally respected other religions and often adopted them. For example, Roman soldiers tended to worship the god Mithras. Mithras came from Persia.
* Everyone in the Empire spoke Latin or Greek. However, the Romans did not force people to give up their own languages.

The army

The army also helped to hold the Empire together. In most regions, people liked having the army nearby. The locals could sell food and other goods to the troops, bringing in money to the region. The army also kept good order. It was also a good career for men from less wealthy families. They could rise through the ranks and reach the rank of centurion. By the third century AD increasing numbers of non-Roman 'barbarians' were serving in the army. Some of them became citizens of the Empire.

Good government and law

The Roman's system of government and law also held the Empire together.

* Roman government and law and order were generally very effective and well organised. By about AD 200 there was a Roman civil service which dealt with the major issues like the law, the army, and collecting taxes.
* The Romans did not bring in officials to run the territories of the Empire. They appointed governors of each province, who were usually soldiers. However, day to day government was usually carried out by local chieftains. As long as provinces paid taxes, kept order and supported the army, emperors usually left them alone.

KEY WORDS

Centurion
Citizenship
Frontier
Judge
Uniformity

SOURCE 1 ▼

By the Roman writer Aelius Aristides writing in the first century AD. To the Romans, the word barbarian did not mean savage like it does today. It simply meant a foreigner, or someone who did not speak their language. Many barbarians lived inside the Empire, especially as auxiliary cavalry soldiers in the army (see page 22).

1

 There is nothing like Roman citizenship in the records of all mankind. Neither sea nor intervening continent are bars to citizenship, nor are Asia and Europe divided in their treatment here [in Rome]. No one worthy of rule or trust remains an alien. The barbarians you educate, rather mildly or sternly according to the nature that each has, because it is right that those who are rulers of men be not inferior to those who are trainers of horses, and that they have tested their natures and guide them accordingly.

- Roman law was very impressive. If a Roman citizen was accused of a crime, they were tried by a judge. However, the citizen could appeal to the emperor if they felt the trial was not fair.

Trade, towns and luxury

The Romans certainly did not invent towns. However, they did take town life to new levels. Trade made people prosperous. Rome traded with China (silk), India (spices) and Africa (wheat and animals). Roman coins have been found all over the Empire and outside it as well. Inside the Empire, the main trade was in slaves and wine. However, merchants made a lot of money out of clothing, jewellery, pottery, timber and marble. Only successful trade like this could provide the money for the Romans' three biggest luxuries: villas (see Source 5 on page 25), baths (see Source 10 on page 27) and amphitheatre games (see pages 37 and 38).

Land and luxury

Most people in the Roman Empire lived and worked in the countryside. The wealthiest people were landlords who lived in large luxurious villas. Landlords made great profits supplying food to the towns. Archaeological studies in northern France have shown that farming was very intensive. Archaeologists have also discovered that many farms were in isolated areas and had no defences. This suggests that life in Roman Gaul was safe and stable.

Life in the towns and cities could be pleasant as well. At the height of the Pax Romana there were about 120 days of holiday each year. People loved to spend these holidays at the games in the amphitheatre or at chariot races (see Source 6 on page 8). Citizens across the Empire enjoyed the security, wealth and stability that the Empire provided.

SOURCE 2 ▼

An extract from An Illustrated History of Europe, *published in 2001. This book was produced by 14 European historians, trying to give a balanced view of different aspects of European history.*

2

❛ **Unity without uniformity: that seems the best description of the Roman Empire in its heyday. The Empire was a sort of federation of cities, under the control of Rome and the emperor, leaving to each of them real autonomy [freedom to govern], so that they could enjoy the benefits of the Pax Romana without being under too heavy a control. In this way the conqueror won over his former enemies with such success that he offered them Roman citizenship. Hence the solidity of the Empire.** ❜

1 Look back at your work for the Brain work activity on page 27. How many of your possible reasons (hypotheses) have been confirmed or strengthened by the information on these pages?

2 What new reasons for Pax Romana have you come across?

3 You have been asked to rearrange pages 24 to 29 so that the words and pictures are more mixed up. Which picture sources would you put in which text sections?

4 List reasons why barbarian tribes living just outside Rome's frontiers might want to become part of the Roman Empire.

Was Pax Romana perfect?

You may have got the impression from pages 24 to 29 that Pax Romana was perfect! However, for most people, it was far from perfect.

Slavery

Slavery was one of the main reasons for the luxury which many Romans enjoyed. The Romans did not invent slavery. However, they depended very heavily on slaves. Slaves were usually prisoners taken from people defeated by Roman armies. Sometimes they were criminals. Some Romans were sold into slavery for offences like not paying debts.

Around one third of the population of Italy were slaves during the Pax Romana period. Slaves worked the fields to grow food. The government used them to build public buildings like Trajan's Forum or the baths at Caracalla. Slave labourers were worked hard. They were often branded on their foreheads or faces. This meant there was little chance of escape. If they did try to escape, punishments received on recapture were often very cruel. Slaves had no protection under the law and were not given Roman citizenship.

Well-educated slaves were usually treated better. They served as doctors, teachers or librarians. Slaves were also used in rich households as maids, cleaners, cooks, hairdressers and security guards. In Pax Romana the treatment of slaves improved slightly, and the number of freedmen increased. Freedmen were usually freed because of good service to their masters. Many freed women married their former masters. Freed slaves enjoyed full rights as citizens of Rome.

1	What evidence is there that slaves were important to Rome?
2	How were slaves treated?
3	Read Source 1. What impression does this source give about the treatment of slaves?

The poorer classes

The main problem for historians studying the poorer classes is that there is very little evidence about them. Very few people lived in luxurious villas and Romans did not write about or paint pictures of ordinary people! From what we do know, life for most people in the Roman Empire was probably similar to life before the Romans. About 90 per cent of the population lived in the countryside working on farms. Most rented their farms from the landlords in the villas. Ordinary British farmers probably lived in huts similar to those in Source 2 on page 25. Others lived in dormitories or small houses built by the landlord.

KEY WORDS
Brand
Jew
Rebellion
Slavery

SOURCE 1 ▼
These are the views of the Roman lawyer, Gaius, on slavery. He was writing in about AD 161.

❝ In our day neither Roman citizens nor any other of those who are under the rule of the Roman people are allowed to treat their slaves unduly harshly and without good reason. The Emperor Antoninus [AD 138–161] decreed that a master who kills a slave is wrong. He also decreed that if the severity of a slave's master was excessive they should be forced to sell their slaves. ❞

City dwellers were generally better off than people in the countryside. Most families even had a slave. However, for the poorest, life was still tough. In Rome, for example, most people lived in packed blocks of flats (see Source 2). The slum district of Subura was well known as a place of dirt, disease and crime.

Fires were also a major problem in the towns and cities. So was hunger. The Empire suffered regularly from crop failures and famine was a constant threat. Local officials in the cities gave out free bread and grain to the poor. Many of the poor survived on these handouts and the charity of wealthy Romans.

SOURCE 2 ▲

A model of blocks of flats in the port of Ostia, near Rome. Poorer families would have rented one or two rooms in these blocks. They had no lighting or sanitation.

Finally, there was even a downside to the great Roman army. When the army arrived in an area, it was billeted. This meant that local people had to find food and shelter for the soldiers and their animals. One of the most common complaints of Roman citizens was having to feed and shelter soldiers.

4 Make a list of the differences between the living conditions in Source 2 and some of the luxury you can see in the sources on pages 24 to 27.

5 Look back at your answer to question 4 on page 29. Write a list of points arguing against the view that barbarian tribes would want to become part of the Roman Empire. Which side of the argument is stronger, in your opinion?

Troubles

The Pax Romana period was relatively stable. Even so, there were still some big upsets at this time.

- There were major rebellions. One of the most serious was in Britain. In AD 61 Queen Boudicca rose up against the Romans. In AD 66–70 there was a major revolt by Jews against Roman rule. Both were eventually crushed by Roman forces.
- There were also disputes about religion. The Romans were generally tolerant of other religions. However, they could be harsh against religions which challenged the authority of the Empire. For example, Druids in Gaul and Britain were hunted down because they encouraged resistance to the Romans. Christians and Jews also suffered because they refused to accept the Roman Emperor as a god.

Pax Romana: For or against?

Anicius Ingenuus examined the leg of the trader carefully. The injury was not as bad as it looked. As a doctor he was familiar with this kind of injury. Legionaries often got injured in battle or in training. This time Anicius was not treating a soldier. The injured man's name was Conor.

Info point

Hadrian's Wall

- The Emperor Hadrian followed on from the Emperor Trajan.
- He was a successful soldier and an effective ruler.
- By Hadrian's time, Rome was no longer expanding. Emperors began building fortifications on the borders of the Empire.
- One of the most famous examples was Hadrian's Wall. It ran right across northern England from present-day Newcastle to the River Solway.

Conor was a Scot who lived on the other side of Hadrian's Wall (see the Info point). He was buying horses at the fort and one of the horses had kicked him.

Anicius bandaged him up. Conor thanked him and said: 'One thing I do like about you Romans is the way you look after your troops. Our doctors are not as good as yours. On the other hand, good medicine doesn't make up for losing your freedom, does it?'

Anicius looked at Conor, puzzled. 'What do you mean?' he asked. Conor then went on to explain that the Scots were not ruled by the Romans. They made their own decisions and had their own laws. They did not have to do what a load of Italians told them to do.

Anicius looked at Conor and said: 'I think you have some strange ideas about how the Roman Empire works. Let's go and talk about this.'

Brain work

You have studied a few reconstructions in this section. The conversation above is also a reconstruction (you can read about Anicius in Source 7 on page 26).

Your task is to carry on the reconstruction. You could carry on writing it like a story, or you could work with other students to write a script for a short play. Your aim is to set out the main strengths and weaknesses of Roman rule. Anicius should argue for the positive aspects of Pax Romana, while Conor should argue against it.

Anicius is likely to mention:
- Roman towns and buildings
- wealth
- trade
- luxury
- good government
- laws

and many other points.

Conor will probably mention:
- religion
- rebellions
- being ruled by Italian emperors
- the poor.

You could set the reconstruction in a place where other people might come and join the conversation. For example, you could bring in:
- a slave who works in the fields.
- a slave who works in a villa.
- a centurion based on Hadrian's Wall.
- an auxiliary based on Hadrian's Wall.
- a British merchant who has got rich supplying the army.
- a British farmer who has been cheated by a greedy landlord.
- any other characters who would help liven up your reconstruction.

OVERVIEW

Most of the evidence we have about Roman women suggests that they were not important: men dominated Roman life. However, some evidence challenges this view. Most surprisingly, some of that evidence is connected with the games in the amphitheatre.

KEY WORDS
Asia Minor
Brooch
Burial
Bustum
Gladiator
Incense

Who was the girl in the grave?

In the summer of 2000 archaeologists from the Museum of London were excavating some Roman burials in Great Dover Street. The site was a cemetery for ordinary Romans. They were not expecting to discover anything unusual. Suddenly, they uncovered a grave unlike all the rest. The contents of the grave were so unusual that a TV programme was made about it.

The grave was a bustum dating from about AD 70. A bustum was a burial involving a procession, prayers and a large fire to burn the body. Only wealthy and important people got this kind of burial. The archaeologists were forced to question why the body was not in a graveyard for the upper classes.

More puzzles emerged from the grave as the archaeologists dug and found:

- a large collection of items like brooches, combs and containers of oil. All these items showed that the dead person was wealthy.
- special pine cones used as incense. The only place where these pine trees grew in London was near the amphitheatre.
- a collection of eight lamps. Lamps were expensive. The richest graves usually had only one or two lamps. In the London grave, the lamps had scenes decorated on them. One lamp showed a fallen gladiator (see Source 1a). Another showed the Egyptian god of the underworld, Anubis (see Source 1b). Slaves dressed as Anubis used to clear dead bodies from the amphitheatre.

All the evidence suggested that the person in the grave was a gladiator. Successful gladiators could be wealthy, so that explained the rich grave. Gladiators were popular, but not very well respected. The richest and most powerful Roman people would not have wanted a gladiator as a neighbour – even when they were in their graves! This explained why such a wealthy grave was in a graveyard for ordinary people.

SOURCE 1a–c ▶
Items from the grave in Great Dover Street.
1a A lamp. The gladiator on the left has fallen in combat and is holding up his hand. The damaged part of the lamp shows an opponent over him, about to finish him off.
1b A lamp showing Anubis, the Egyptian god of the dead.
1c The remaining burnt bones of the body.

SOURCE 2 ▼
A wall carving from Halikarnassos in modern-day Turkey showing female gladiators. Turkey was in the Roman province of Asia Minor.

SOURCE 3 ▶
The Roman writer Tacitus writing in AD 63. Like most upper-class Romans, he went to the games but did not think gladiators were respectable.

1a

1b

1c

There was one final twist. After analysing the bones, the archaeologists discovered that the body was that of a woman. A female gladiator! This was a really important find. Roman sources did mention female gladiators (see Sources 2 and 3), but no body or any other archaeological evidence had ever been found to prove this.

> **The Emperor Nero staged many gladiatorial shows in his reign. They were as magnificent as any shows which went before. Many women of rank and Senators disgraced themselves by fighting in the arena.**

3

But what did this new evidence mean? What did the female gladiator tell archaeologists about Roman London? What did she reveal about the Roman games? What can she tell us about women in Roman society?

Turn over to investigate these questions yourself!

Brain work

You'd better be absolutely sure. I've never heard of female gladiators. And how can you be sure your grave is the grave of a female gladiator? We'll look silly if we're wrong.

Imagine you are one of the archaeologists on the site at Great Dover Street. This is your boss, Davina. You want to tell the media about the female gladiator. However, doubting Davina is not sure. She does not want to announce this and then find out that you are wrong.

Use the information and evidence on these pages to put together a short report or presentation for Davina. Your report should convince her:

- that there were female gladiators.
- that the grave in Great Dover Street contained a female gladiator.

Why did the Romans love the games so much?

The centre of every town

The Roman games were a huge feature of Roman life. Romans could go to the theatre or watch chariot races for entertainment, but it was the games in the amphitheatre which were really popular. Every town in the Empire which could afford one had an amphitheatre. The amphitheatre in London could hold 7000 people – about one third of the population of the city at the time. The greatest amphitheatre of them all was the Colosseum in Rome. It could hold about 50,000 people.

KEY WORDS

Adviser
Bestiarii
Colosseum
Murmillone
Mythical
Priestess
Prisoner of war
Retiarii

SOURCE 1a–b ▲
The Colosseum in Rome as it looks today.
1a The outside of the Colosseum.
1b The inside of the Colosseum. The area in the centre was the arena where the gladiators fought. It was originally paved. The walls you can see were underneath the floor of the arena. They were cages for wild animals and rooms where gladiators waited to go into the arena.

SOURCE 2 ◀
A scene from the Hollywood movie Barabbas, *which was made in 1962.*

1 Sources 1 and 2 both show the same building. Make a list of as many differences between the two sources as you can.

2 Explain how Source 1 can help you to decide whether or not Source 2 is an accurate reconstruction.

How did the games become so important?

The original point of the games was religious. Rich Romans organised fights between their slaves as a tribute to a dead friend or family member. They believed that the blood of the slave who died would guide his rich owner after death. The first recorded fight was in 264 BC.

Over the next hundred years these fights changed. The Romans began staging them in amphitheatres where spectators could watch. The reason for this was a combination of entertainment and punishment. Criminals, prisoners of war, disobedient slaves or anyone who offended the emperor were all sent to die in the arena. <u>Sometimes they were sent to be killed by wild animals.</u> Sometimes they were given <u>weapons to fight the animals.</u> They were often given a sword (a gladius) and forced to fight other criminals or prisoners.

Eventually the emperors took control of the games in Rome. They controlled the gladiator schools and planned the events. The emperors knew that staging games made them popular with the people. <u>The emperor sat in his own box to watch the games, with his family and closest advisers around him.</u> As the people in Rome could see that the emperor liked the games as well, he appeared to be one of them. The games also made Romans feel proud of their Empire. The games reminded them that Rome ruled an empire which contained Scottish wildcats, Asian tigers and <u>African elephants!</u> A good example of an emperor who saw the value of the games was Trajan. He once organised games which lasted 123 days and involved over 9000 gladiators, animal trainers and guards.

3 Where do you think the word 'gladiator' came from?

4 Explain why the emperors spent so much money on providing games.

37

What were the games like?

The usual format for the games was to have an animal hunt in the morning. Wild animals were captured from all over the Empire and brought to the games in Rome. They were let loose into the arena. <u>Specialist gladiators called bestiarii then fought and killed the animals.</u>

In the afternoon there would be combats between gladiators. By Trajan's time gladiators were specially trained slaves. Some free Roman men and women actually volunteered to become gladiators. It was risky, of course, but successful gladiators became wealthy and famous. We know that some retired peacefully after a career in the arena.

To make the fights more entertaining, gladiators fought in different styles:

- <u>Retiarii fought with tridents (three-pronged forks) and nets.</u>
- <u>Murmillones carried a gladius, helmet and square shield.</u>
- Thracians fought with curved daggers and small round shields.

As time went on, the games got bigger and more spectacular. The organisers tried out more and more new ideas. They searched hard for new animals – even giraffes appeared in the arena. They then organised fights between animals (for example, between bears and bulls). They flooded the Colosseum and staged sea battles. One of the most popular spectacles was the recreation of mythical events and characters from countries the Romans had conquered.

SOURCE 3 ▲
A Roman mosaic from around AD 150.

SOURCE 4 ▼
A wall carving from Asia Minor. The emperor is presenting the winner's crown.

SOURCE 5 ▶
A wall carving showing a gladiator killing a bull.

SOURCE 6 ▼
A mosaic from Sicily showing a rhinoceros hunt.

SOURCE 7 ▶
A wall carving showing gladiators fighting wild animals.

SOURCE 8 ▶
A mosaic found in North Africa showing a gladiator being killed by an animal.

Brain work

A major Hollywood studio is making a movie about Ancient Rome. They are planning some scenes which show the Colosseum. A researcher for the film has found Sources 3–8 on pages 38 and 39, which show events at the Colosseum, but she is having trouble interpreting them. She is not sure what is happening in each scene.

See if you can help her to interpret the sources.

- *Hint 1*: Look at Source 9 to see how a professional historian can interpret a source.
- *Hint 2*: On page 37, some sections are underlined. These sections might give you some ideas.
- *Hint 3*: You could use a table like the one below to record your thoughts. Alternatively, you could just choose one source and analyse it in the same way that Source 9 has been analysed.

Source	Brief description	What this source shows is...	Extra comments
3			
4			
5			
6			
7			
8			

Where did women fit into the games?

Women in the stadium

So, where did women fit into the scene at the games? This is a tricky question to answer. Let's start with the spectators. If you had been in the Colosseum, you would have seen the emperor in his private box with several women nearby. They were Vestal Virgins – Roman priestesses. However, to find any more women you would have had to look in the worst seats right at the back of the stadium. Even wealthy women had to sit with the poor, except for the emperor's family.

Novelty act or top of the bill?

What about down in the arena? Historians are not sure how important women gladiators were. It depends on how you interpret the evidence. Some historians think female gladiators were a novelty act, just something different to draw in the crowds. However, one leading historian thinks they were more important than this.

Professor Kathleen Coleman is a professor at Harvard University in the USA. She was the historical adviser for the Hollywood movie *Gladiator*, which was released in 2000. She has made a detailed study of evidence like the wall carving from Halikarnassos (see Source 9).

SOURCE 9 ▶
A wall carving from Halikarnassos in modern-day Turkey, with notes showing how Professor Kathleen Coleman interpreted it.

Women are equipped with full gladiator weapons and armour. This suggests that they were proper warriors and not a novelty act.

They are in the proper fighting stance for gladiators, just like men.

Arm guards

Shield

Gladius

9

Their helmets are on the ground. This suggests the two gladiators are exhausted. They have fought to a stalemate and will both live to fight again. This was a common event for the top gladiators.

Brain work

Look back at the advice you gave to the researcher for the Brain work activity on page 40. Add any extra points of information which you have learnt. You could put these in the 'Extra comments' column of your table.

Why have historians' ideas about Roman women changed?

For a long time most historians believed that Roman women were not powerful. One simple reason is health. There was no birth control in Rome. Women often had many children and childbirth could be dangerous. This helps to explain why the average lifespan for Roman women was only 28. Plenty of other evidence seemed to show that men dominated Roman society:

- Look at Source 1. It shows a Roman mother with her baby boy. It was up to the father whether the child would be accepted into the family. If a family could not afford to look after children, they were often left to die. This happened more often to baby girls than to boys. In this source the father is watching the baby being fed before he holds him, which shows that he accepts the child.
- Sources 2 and 5 suggest that the main job of Roman women was simply to look nice or to entertain.
- Sources 3 and 4 suggest that Roman women were second-class citizens.

SOURCE 1 ◀
A wall carving showing Roman parents and their child.

SOURCE 2 ▼
A sculpture showing a fashionable hairstyle for women in Rome. Several skilled slaves would have been needed to create this style. The Romans developed curling tongs, rollers and many of the tools a modern hairdresser uses.

‘ **Still more annoying is the woman who, as soon as she sits down to dinner, talks about poets and poetry, professors, lawyers. Wives should not try to be public speakers. I myself cannot stand a woman who is educated – as if men cared about such things. If she has to correct somebody, let her correct her girl friends and leave her husband alone.** ’

SOURCE 3 ◀
An extract from the writings of Juvenal, AD 110. Juvenal wrote stories criticising many different people and groups in Rome.

❝ **Egnatius Mecennius beat his wife to death with a club, because she had been drinking wine. Not only was he not prosecuted for his actions, but he wasn't even criticised, for everyone agreed that she was a perfect example of someone who had paid the penalty for being drunk. Certainly, any woman who drinks too much wine closes the door to virtue and opens it to sinfulness.** ❞

4

SOURCE 4 ▲

An extract from Memorable Deeds and Sayings *by the Roman writer Valerius Maximus, AD 31.*

SOURCE 5 ▶

Female gymnasts shown in a wall painting from the AD 200s.

Perhaps the strongest evidence to support the view that women were powerless comes from Roman laws. The Romans had many laws relating to women and the family. From these laws we know that:

- the head of every household was the father – the paterfamilias.
- the paterfamilias arranged the marriages of his daughters – he could kill his wife or daughter without being punished.
- a married woman was under the complete control of her husband, including any property she owned.

Other laws also showed what the Romans seemed to think of women:

- Women could not enter the Senate.
- Women could not work as lawyers or judges.
- Women could not vote.

5

spiteful

intolerant   rude

shocking

harsh   loving

cheerful

1   Look carefully at the word bag on the left and the words in it. Make sure you know what the words mean before you tackle the following questions – look in a dictionary or ask your teacher to explain any you do not understand.

2   Which words from the word bag describe the attitude of Source 1 towards women?

3   Which words could be used to describe the attitude of Source 3?

4   List some more words that could be added to the word bag which would be useful for describing how Sources 2, 4 and 5 portray women.

5   'Roman women were not powerful. Men dominated Roman society.' Choose the five strongest pieces of evidence which could be used to support this statement.

Roman women – changing interpretations

Since the 1980s historians have been rethinking their views about Roman women. They still believe that Rome was dominated by men. They still think that male children were valued more highly than girls. However, they now think that women were more important than we used to think they were. There are two main reasons for this change in thinking.

1 New evidence – powerful women

You have already read the story of the female gladiators on pages 34 to 41. Other women also became famous and important in the Roman Empire. The wives of emperors were well-known figures, and some had real power:

- Livia was the wife of the Emperor Augustus (27 BC–AD 14). Sources from the time suggest she had a big influence on how Augustus ran the Empire.

- Faustina was the wife of the Emperor Antoninus Pius (AD 138–161). She was well known for her work with charities. One of her good causes was Roman girls from poor families – she paid for their education.

- Julia Domna was the wife of the Emperor Septimius Severus (AD 193–211). Severus was involved in wars for much of his reign, and he left Julia in charge. She proved to be an excellent ruler. She also advised her son Caracalla during his reign as emperor (AD 211–217).

Women were also successful in business:

- In Pompeii, archaeologists discovered a brick-making business owned by a woman called Eumachia. She was wealthy enough to have paid for several public buildings to be constructed.

- Another example can be found in Gaul. A businesswoman called Melania owned large farms in many parts of the Empire and had 24,000 slaves.

All of these were exceptional individuals. What about ordinary women in normal families? The traditional view was that Roman husbands controlled their wives. However, we now know that Roman men and women could get divorced fairly easily. Women in Britain still struggled to get divorces in the early twentieth century. But most Roman marriages did not end in divorce. A lot of evidence suggests that Roman marriages were more like partnerships.

SOURCE 6 ▼

A coin showing the head of Julia Domna. Being on a coin was a mark of great respect and prestige.

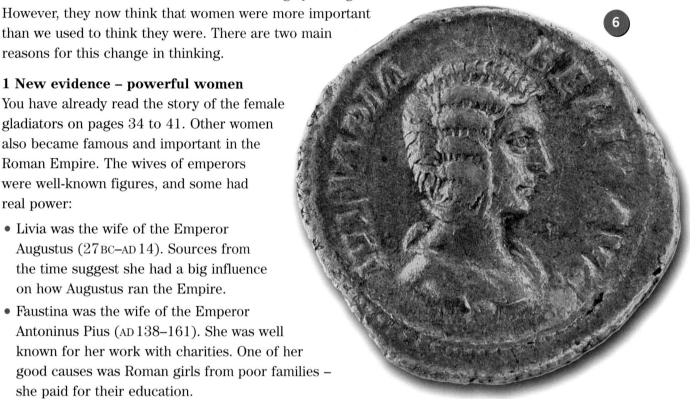

SOURCE 7 ▲

An unfinished carving on a Roman tomb which shows love between a man and a woman.

2 New ways of looking at the old evidence – Roman families

The main sources of information on Roman women were the laws set out to govern women and the family. Historians have started to wonder whether these laws were actually followed. Source 8 sums up the new thinking.

SOURCE 8 ▶

An extract from The Roman World Sourcebook, *a university textbook by Professor David Cherry. It was published in 2001.*

❝ It is doubtful that the traditional picture of the Roman household actually fits the reality of Roman family life. The traditional image comes from documents describing Roman laws. But legal rules rarely described what actually happened in practice. Literary sources and inscriptions from funerals suggest what really mattered to Romans was the family. What mattered were the relationships of husband and wife, parent and child. ❞

8

Finally, historians have asked themselves about family life today. Does the average family today exist because of the law? Or is it because they live together and love each other? Why should the Romans have been any different?

SOURCE 9 ▶

An extract from a marriage contract of about AD 13. *A dowry was a gift which the parents gave to their daughter when she got married so that she brought some wealth into her marriage.*

❝ Thermion [the wife] and Appollonius [the husband] agree that they have come together for the purposes of sharing their lives with one another. Appollonius agrees that he has received from Thermion some gold as a dowry. From now on he will furnish her with all necessities and clothing that he can afford. He will not mistreat her or cast her out or insult her or bring in another wife. Thermion will fulfil her duties towards her husband and her marriage. She will not damage their common home and will not consort with another man. ❞

9

Brain work

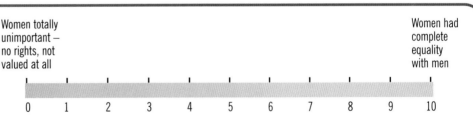

Women totally unimportant – no rights, not valued at all

Women had complete equality with men

0 1 2 3 4 5 6 7 8 9 10

1 Where do you think the traditional view of Roman women should fit on the above interpretation scale?

2 Look at the information on these pages. Decide where to put the more recent thinking of historians on the scale.

3 Produce a short presentation explaining why there is a gap on your scale. You need to explain:

   a at least two points that describe what the traditional view of Roman women was.

   b at least two examples of the evidence that gave rise to that view.

   c at least two ways in which historians have changed their views.

   d at least two reasons why historians have changed their views.

   e at least one way in which historians have not changed their minds.

OVERVIEW

Historians disagree about the date of the fall of Rome, the reasons for the fall and even whether Rome really fell at all. This is your chance to study why they disagree so much.

Did the barbarians kill the Roman Empire?

In AD 476 the last Roman emperor fell. Source 1 gives the impression that the barbarians suddenly swarmed into Rome in one attack and destroyed the Empire. In fact, the story is longer and more complicated than that.

Barbarians had been attacking Rome since AD 166. They wanted gold, slaves and any other valuables they could take. They were not the only ones. In the late 200s and early 300s Rome faced raids from barbarians in the West and the Persian Empire in the East. Emperors often faced wars at opposite ends of the Empire (see Source 2).

SOURCE 1 ▲

The city of Rome is attacked by the barbarian Goths in AD 410. Rome was attacked several times in the 400s. This picture was drawn in the late 1800s. People in Britain at that time were fascinated by the Roman Empire. This was probably because they saw similarities between the British Empire and the Roman Empire.

SOURCE 2 ◄

The main movements of the barbarian nations in the 400s. There were many different barbarian peoples. The Romans tended to call them all Germani because they lived in the region the Romans called Germania.

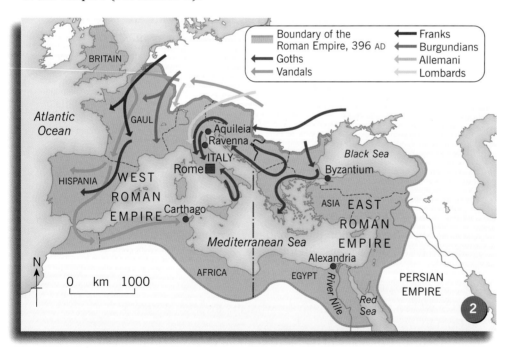

By the late 300s the Roman Empire was in decline. By now the barbarians were no longer raiding; they were migrating. They wanted to settle on the rich lands of the Roman Empire. They were also being driven westwards by another fierce barbarian people called the Huns.

KEY WORDS

Deposed
Goths
Huns
Migrating

SOURCE 3 ▶

The main barbarian kingdoms which emerged after the fall of Rome.

The Emperor Theodosius realised this. He could not keep all the barbarians out. He decided to allow some barbarians in so that they could help keep other barbarians out. He allowed the Goths to settle in the Empire. Other barbarians, including Franks and Vandals, were also allowed to settle in the Empire. Many Goths (about 20,000) joined the Roman army. However, they kept their own language and customs. They did not adopt Roman ideas the way the people had done in the Pax Romana (see pages 24 to 33). As a result, they were not as loyal to Rome as people had been in the Pax Romana.

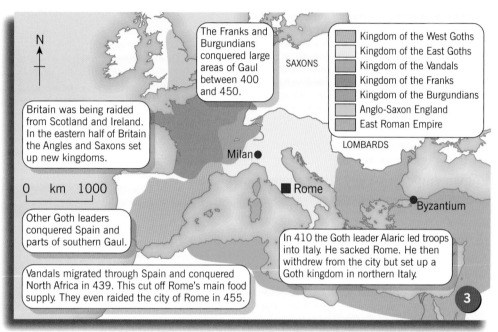

The Franks and Burgundians conquered large areas of Gaul between 400 and 450.

Britain was being raided from Scotland and Ireland. In the eastern half of Britain the Angles and Saxons set up new kingdoms.

Other Goth leaders conquered Spain and parts of southern Gaul.

Vandals migrated through Spain and conquered North Africa in 439. This cut off Rome's main food supply. They even raided the city of Rome in 455.

In 410 the Goth leader Alaric led troops into Italy. He sacked Rome. He then withdrew from the city but set up a Goth kingdom in northern Italy.

Kingdom of the West Goths
Kingdom of the East Goths
Kingdom of the Vandals
Kingdom of the Franks
Kingdom of the Burgundians
Anglo-Saxon England
East Roman Empire

SAXONS

LOMBARDS

Milan

Rome

Byzantium

0 km 1000

In AD 395 the Emperor Theodosius divided the Empire into East and West. The Eastern Empire fought off its enemies and continued to last. It had always been the stronger half of the Empire. It was richer and had a larger population.

On the other hand, the Western Empire was falling apart by the early 400s. It simply could not cope with the huge numbers of barbarians looking to carve out new kingdoms for themselves on former Roman lands.

By AD 476 the Roman Empire had shrunk so much it had virtually disappeared. It consisted of the city of Rome and parts of Italy. In AD 476 the Goth leader Odoacer became king of Italy and officially deposed the last Roman emperor.

I always wondered why the Roman Empire fell, and now I know. The barbarians were one main cause of the fall of Rome. I wonder if there were any more causes.

1 Why did the barbarians raid the Roman Empire?

2 Why was Rome in crisis in the late 200s and early 300s?

3 a Why did the raids turn into migrations?

   b Why was this an important development?

4 a List three examples of the barbarians conquering former Roman territories.

   b List two reasons why they were able to do this by the 400s.

Did the Romans kill the Roman Empire?

Did the Romans kill the Roman Empire? This might seem like a strange question. However, many historians think that the Empire became weaker from about AD 250 onwards. They believe that Rome's weakness made it possible for the barbarians to successfully attack Rome.

Too many emperors

The Romans never agreed on a way of replacing one emperor with another. This often led to bitter arguments and even civil wars over who would be emperor. For example, in AD 259 there were 18 men who claimed to be the emperor. Even when an emperor was accepted, his chances of staying in power were not good. Between AD 350 and 476 there were 25 Roman emperors. Only six of them managed to rule for more than ten years.

A cash crisis

By the 300s Rome was facing major financial problems. You have read about the luxury of the Pax Romana on pages 24 to 29. The games, baths, temples and other wonderful buildings all cost a fortune. Upper-class Romans continued to buy goods from India, China and the eastern half of the Empire. At the same time, the western half of the Empire was not making as much money as it was spending. The result was that the Western Empire started to run out of money. This was serious. Money was needed to pay for the legions and to maintain the fortifications on the frontiers (see Source 2).

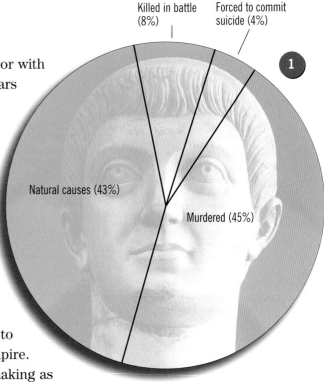

Killed in battle (8%)
Forced to commit suicide (4%)
Natural causes (43%)
Murdered (45%)

SOURCE 1 ▲
Cause of death of Roman emperors in the period AD 250–476.

Emperors tried to solve this problem by raising taxes. The taxes fell heavily on the poorer and middle-class Romans who ran businesses. Eventually, many citizens found themselves too poor to pay taxes. More and more people started to depend on the dole – handouts of bread and grain. This cost money and made the cash crisis even worse. The Roman upper classes avoided paying taxes by moving out of the cities. They started living in large fortified villas in the countryside. They hired their own soldiers to frighten off tax collectors. As a result, the towns declined. This meant that trade declined. This meant that the emperors lost even more tax money.

The army

The mighty Roman army also began to decline:

- The frontiers of the Empire were very long. The army was thinly stretched guarding those frontiers.
- As Roman government began to decline, the army was less reliable because it was not paid regularly. Men were less willing to fight if they were not certain of being paid.
- More seriously, by the 300s very few Romans were prepared to serve in the army. There were plenty of other (easier) ways to make a good living. Upper-class Romans no longer wanted to serve as officers. Most ordinary soldiers came from the poorest classes, or they were barbarians.
- The barbarians were good soldiers, but they were less loyal to Rome than the old legions had been. Rome relied too heavily on barbarian soldiers to keep out other barbarians from the Empire!

1. Look at Source 1. Explain how this chart shows that Rome suffered from an unstable government between AD 250 and 476.

2. Explain how the Emperor Theodosius weakened the Western Empire.

3. a Would you say that the cash crisis was more serious than the decline of the army?

   b In what ways were these two problems connected?

   c Is there a connection between the decline of the army and the barbarians?

Therefore, there were other factors as well as the barbarians which explain the fall of Rome. Divisions within the Empire and money are big factors.

Did Christianity kill the Roman Empire?

During the first century AD, Christianity was a small but growing religion. By the early 300s it was the main religion of the poorer classes in the Empire. Many upper-class Romans, especially women, also became Christians. In AD 323 the Emperor Constantine became a Christian. Constantine hoped that all Romans would become Christians too. He hoped that this would unite the Empire. By the late 300s Christianity was the official religion of the Empire.

One historian, Edward Gibbon, believed that this damaged Rome badly. Gibbon is probably the best-known writer on the fall of the Roman Empire. You will study him in more depth on pages 52 and 53. He believed that:

- Christianity was basically a religion of peace. Gibbon thought that Christianity weakened the will of the Roman people to fight wars to defend themselves.

- Christians built many beautiful churches, for example St Peter's Church in Rome (right). Gibbon thought that this used up valuable cash which was needed to defend the Empire.

- Christianity tried to ban other religions. This led to wars within the Empire as followers of other religions defended their beliefs.

- Christians had many arguments amongst themselves. Emperors found themselves trying to sort out disputes among Christians instead of concentrating on running the Empire (right).

So, there are more factors to consider. It appears the decline of the Roman Empire was speeded up by Constantine's decision to become a Christian.

1   Why did Constantine become a Christian?

2   Explain how the Emperor Constantine weakened the Western Empire.

3   Is Source 1 convincing evidence to support all of Edward Gibbon's views?

4   Try to memorise the reasons Edward Gibbon gave for believing Christianity damaged Rome. You could write a short poem or draw a diagram to help you.

Did nature kill the Roman Empire?

KEY WORDS

Bishop
Malaria
Persecute
Plague

SOURCE 1 ◀

The palace of the Christian Bishop Theodore at Aquilea in northern Italy. It was built in the mid 300s

SOURCE 2 ▼

A mosaic of the palace of the Goth leader Theodoric in Ravenna, northern Italy. Theodoric followed Odoacer as king of Italy.

Could the weather have destroyed the Roman Empire? In 1917 a historian called Ellsworth Huntington put forward this view. He believed that the weather became drier in the later Roman period. This forced the Romans to build more reservoirs and ditches to irrigate fields. This provided a breeding ground for mosquitoes. These insects then spread malaria and other diseases across the Empire.

The Empire was hit by devastating plagues in the second and third centuries. One writer tells of a plague which killed 5000 people a day. The plagues reduced the population of the Empire dramatically. This meant there were fewer Romans to serve in the army, to produce food and materials to trade, and to pay taxes. There were also many bad harvests in the later Roman period as the weather became drier.

Based on this evidence, it seems that natural factors also helped to bring down the Roman Empire.

Did the Roman Empire really die?

It is worth remembering that some historians feel that the Roman Empire did not really 'fall'. They point out that the Eastern Empire did not fall. In fact, it lasted another 1000 years. They also say that the barbarian kings who conquered the Empire admired Rome in many ways. They kept their own identity, but they also adopted many Roman ideas. Their laws, language and religion were all affected by Rome. In a way, they simply continued Rome, but with their own additions and under a different name.

1. Explain the connection between plague, taxes and the army.
2. Look at Source 2. How can you tell that the Goth leader Theodoric admired the Romans even though his people had conquered Italy?

Conclusion on the fall of Rome: Did Edward Gibbon get it right?

You have already come across Edward Gibbon on page 50. He was a very important historian, even though he wrote his book about the fall of the Empire over 200 years ago (see the Info point).

Gibbon's ideas

Gibbon did not see the barbarians as the main reason for the fall of Rome. He believed that the barbarians succeeded because three factors fatally weakened the Roman Empire.

- The spread of Christianity weakened the Roman Empire.
- The Roman Empire was weakened by too much luxury.
- The Empire was badly run by its emperors.

Most historians still accept Gibbon's ideas. However, they do not agree completely:

- Many do not agree with Gibbon's views about which factors were the most important in causing the fall of the Empire.
- Other historians think he let his personal views in the 1770s influence his judgements about the history of Rome.

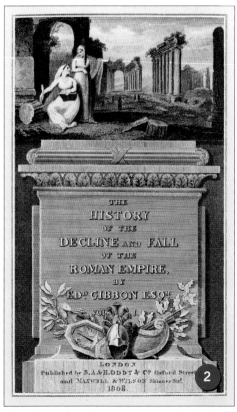

Info point

Edward Gibbon

- *Historians looking at the fall of Rome always starts with a book called* The History of the Decline and Fall of the Roman Empire *by Edward Gibbon.*

- *Gibbon was born in 1737, the son of an English country gentleman.*

- *He went to Oxford University at the age of 15.*

- *For many years he could not decide what he wanted to do in life. Then he visited the ruins of Rome in 1764. He was so taken by what he saw that he decided to research and write a great history of the Empire.*

- *Gibbon served as an MP from 1781 to 1783. In Britain at that time the king had to listen to parliament. In most states, kings and emperors ignored parliaments. Gibbon thought the British system was much better. He hated the idea of kings, queens or emperors having too much power.*

- *His book,* The History of the Decline and Fall of the Roman Empire, *was first published in 1776. It was very successful. It was also praised by other historians because of the enormous amount of research Gibbon had done.*

- *Gibbon used a very large range of original sources to research his book. This was unusual in those days.*

SOURCE 1 ◀
A portrait of historian Edward Gibbon.

SOURCE 2 ◀
The frontispiece of Gibbon's book.

Wow! There were lots of events that contributed to the fall of the Roman Empire. It's difficult to decide which was the most important.

Brain work

Imagine you are a writer and your publishers have decided to publish an updated version of Edward Gibbon's book. They want some advice from you on how to bring Gibbon's ideas up to date.

Stage 1: Start by getting your own ideas clear

1 Draw a diagram to sum up what you have learnt on pages 46–52. A possible diagram is set out below, but you may have a better idea.

2 Once you have drawn your diagram, add extra examples which show how each factor weakened the Roman Empire. We have started one, for barbarians, but there are plenty of others.

3 See if you can find any connections between factors. If you can, draw a line joining them together and label the line to show what the connection is. We have suggested one connection but there are many more.

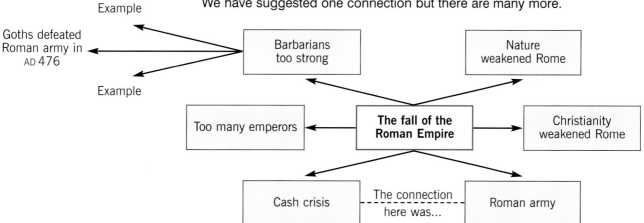

Stage 2: Report back to your publishers

You now need to report back to your publishers about Gibbon's book. Your report needs to look at these questions:

• Do you agree that Gibbon's three factors were important?

• Did Gibbon miss out any factors which you think need to be added?

• Do you agree with Gibbon about which were the most important factors?

• Is there any evidence that Gibbon's personal views influenced his judgements about Rome?

• What other factors (for example, connections) need to be added to Gibbon's book to bring it up to date?

You could present your ideas as a written report or a presentation.

The medieval period in two pages!

Norman	William I	1066–1087
	William II	1087–1100
	Henry I	1100–1135
	Stephen	1135–1154
Angevin	Henry II	1154–1189
	Richard I	1189–1199
	John	1199–1216
Plantagenet	Henry III	1216–1272
	Edward I	1272–1307
	Edward II	1307–1327
	Edward III	1327–1377
	Richard II	1377–1399
Lancastrian	Henry IV	1399–1413
	Henry V	1413–1422
	Henry VI	1422–1461
Yorkist	Edward IV	1461–1483
	Edward V	1483–1483
	Richard III	1483–1485
Tudor	Henry VII	1485–1509

KEY WORDS

Baron
Conquer
Government
Medieval
Monarch
Norman Conquest
Normandy
Official
Peasant
Ruler

What is the medieval period?

It is not easy to cram the medieval period, 1066–1500, into two pages!
There were many important people, events and developments that should
be included but they cannot all be covered in detail here. In these two
pages we are going to look briefly at the families of monarchs who ruled
England in this period.

The first major event of this period was the Norman Conquest, when the
Duke of Normandy in France successfully invaded England. The Conquest
began in 1066 but it was another five or six years before the Normans
really controlled England. Norman rule brought some big changes. By
1087 most of the English lords had been replaced by Normans.

The lords and kings who came after William the Conqueror saw themselves
as French *and* English lords. They were determined to keep their lands on
either side of the Channel. For much of the 1100s most of these lords and
monarchs probably cared more about their French lands. By the late 1200s
this was beginning to change. From the 1200s to the 1400s there were
many wars between the rulers of England and the French kings. One of
them lasted from about 1340 to 1440. This is called the Hundred Years
War. Kings of England became more focused on their lands in England than

SOURCE 1 ▼
*King Henry I using one of the
cross-Channel ferries which were
set up by English kings. English
monarchs and their officials were
constantly crossing the Channel.*

their lands in France. By the mid 1400s virtually all the English monarch's French lands had been lost to the French kings.

Shortly before 1066 relations between England and its neighbours were fairly peaceful. This changed as well during the medieval period. In the 1170s Henry II took his forces to Ireland. In the 1290s Edward I conquered Wales. He tried to conquer Scotland soon after. From that point on there were many wars. England was the most powerful country in Britain and Ireland. Despite this, by 1500 neither Ireland nor Scotland was under English control.

William I was able to conquer England at the start of the medieval period with the help of his powerful family and his barons. But not all the monarchs were able to control their families and barons and the period 1066–1500 saw many bitter civil wars. Civil wars are struggles between monarchs and the people. Some of the most serious civil wars were in the reign of Stephen in the 1130s. There were still brutal wars going on in the 1400s – the Wars of the Roses. These were struggles between the House (family) of Lancaster and the House of York to control the country.

Another important area to think about when studying the medieval period is religion. For most ordinary medieval people, kings and peasants alike, religion was the most important thing in their lives (you will study this on pages 72 to 75). Monarchs built new churches and protected the Church. The Church was also important because it played a central role in making the government run properly. Several monarchs tried to control the Church. This led to major arguments in the 1090s, 1160s and in the early 1200s. After this time, the were no major disagreements between monarchs and the Church.

Brain work

The paragraphs on these pages have no headings. Here are some suggested headings:

- Barons.
- From French to English kings.
- Relations with Wales, Scotland and Ireland.
- Religion.
- The Norman Conquest.

1 Decide which heading belongs with which paragraph. Better still, come up with more exciting and interesting headings for each paragraph.

2 Write your paragraph headings on some cards. On the back of each card, write down the main changes which took place during the period. If there are no changes, note down the factors which stayed the same.

3 There is only space for two pictures on these pages. Have a look through this unit and suggest which other picture sources could go on these pages if there was another page to fill.

KEY WORDS
Adviser
Archer
Bishop
Cavalry
Duke
Earl
Historian
Knight
Lord
Monk

OVERVIEW

The Norman Conquest of 1066 changed medieval Europe. A new cross-Channel empire was born. In this section you are going to study the impact of this development on England, France and England's other neighbours as well.

How did William the Conqueror create a Norman empire in 1066?

Fast-forward: The funeral of William the Conqueror, September 1087

In July 1087 William was leading his armies in France. He was trying to stop the French king taking some of his lands in Normandy. Near the city of Mantes he was badly injured. In September he died from his wounds. His family and friends planned a magnificent funeral for him in the church of St Stephen at Caen in Normandy. William had built this church. The plan was for William to be buried in the church, while a bishop read out a short speech about William's life. The scene might have looked something like the picture below.

Unfortunately, this is not what happened. William had put on a lot of weight in his last few years. His coffin was not big enough. His body burst as they tried to stuff it into the coffin. The resulting smell was awful. All the mourners ran out of the church. A few poor monks had to hold their noses and finish the service.

Today, this story seems a bit gruesome, maybe even a bit funny. People in medieval times probably thought this too. However, they may have thought other things as well.

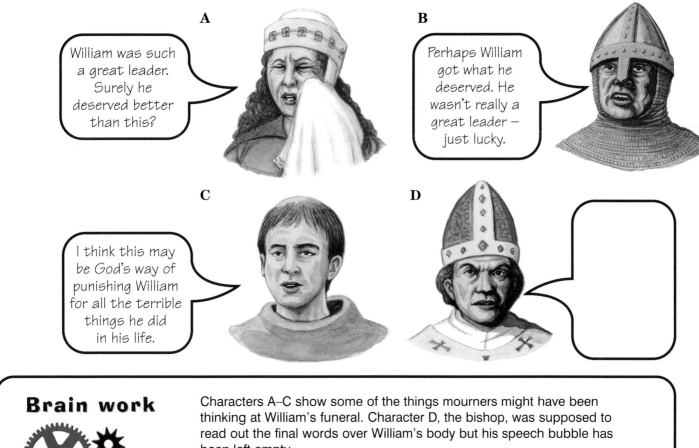

A — William was such a great leader. Surely he deserved better than this?

B — Perhaps William got what he deserved. He wasn't really a great leader – just lucky.

C — I think this may be God's way of punishing William for all the terrible things he did in his life.

D —

Brain work

Characters A–C show some of the things mourners might have been thinking at William's funeral. Character D, the bishop, was supposed to read out the final words over William's body but his speech bubble has been left empty.

At the end of this section (on page 67) you are going to rewrite history a little. You are going to imagine you are the bishop and you will write a short speech so you get the chance to say some words over William's body.

For now, work through pages 57–67 carefully. Take some notes and make up your own mind about William. When you have done your research, you will decide what you would have said if you were the bishop.

So, did William deserve a better send-off? Let's look at his life and career.

William's early life

By 1066 William was very familiar with hardship, danger and war. One of his greatest achievements was surviving as Duke of Normandy. He was only 7 years old when he became Duke. Throughout his childhood he faced plots from other Norman barons who wanted to take his place. Several of his close advisers were murdered. He only survived because his father's friends looked after him. Many times he had to hide in the cottages of peasants as enemies came looking for him. Even as a grown man he was often in danger. He was almost constantly at war from 1047 to 1060.

Not surprisingly, he became a tough and able leader. This helped him with his greatest achievement: the conquest of England.

The conquest of England

In January 1066 the English king, Edward the Confessor, died with no son to follow him. Three men claimed the throne of England:

- The king of Norway, Harald Hardrada. He was descended from the Viking kings who had ruled England from 1016 to 1042.
- An English earl, Harold Godwinson. He was the most powerful Saxon earl (English nobleman). He claimed that Edward had promised him the throne as he lay on his deathbed.
- Duke William of Normandy. Edward the Confessor had grown up in Normandy. Most of his friends were Normans. William claimed that Edward had promised the throne to him in 1051.

All three men had some kind of claim. But this dispute would not be settled in a court. Instead, it would be settled by war.

In the end, the events favoured William. For most of the first part of 1066, William built up an army in Normandy. However, for a large part of the summer he was unable to cross the Channel because the wind was blowing the wrong way. He was frustrated, but he was a good commander. He kept calm and patient, and waited for the right conditions.

SOURCE 1 ◀

A scene from the Bayeux Tapestry showing William's men loading his ships ready for the invasion. The Bayeux Tapestry was produced after the Norman Conquest and tells the story of the events of the period 1050–1066.

On the English side of the Channel, Harold Godwinson waited for William. Then, in September, Harald Hardrada landed in northern England. Harold Godwinson rushed north and defeated Hardrada in a bloody battle at Stamford Bridge in Yorkshire.

SOURCE 2 ▲

A scene from the Bayeux Tapestry showing the death of Harold Godwinson at the Battle of Hastings.

Luckily for William, the wind changed direction while Harold was in the north. He was able to land on the south coast without opposition. When Harold heard about the Norman invasion, he cursed his luck. His troops were tired after hard fighting and long marching. Should he fight William now, or should he wait until he had fresh troops? In the end, he decided to fight.

Many historians think this was a mistake. Harold met William at Senlac Field, near Hastings on the south coast of England, in October 1066. It was a long and bloody battle. William used his troops cleverly, especially his archers and cavalry. Eventually, Harold Godwinson was killed and the English forces were defeated.

William was clever enough to know that this one battle was not going to win England. In the next two months he marched through Sussex and Kent, burning towns and terrorising people. He wanted the English to be afraid of him. He eventually reached London and was crowned king of England on Christmas Day 1066.

SOURCE 3 ▲

A painting showing William the Conqueror's coronation in 1066. The painting dates from the nineteenth century.

William must have felt satisfied. He had created an empire in just a few months. But were his troubles just beginning? Turn over and see!

1 What evidence supports the view that William the Conqueror was tough?

2 Many historians have commented that William was a lucky ruler. What evidence supports this?

3 What other factors can you find in this section which explain William's success in 1066?

4 Look again at Source 3. Imagine there is a speech bubble coming from William's head. What words would you write in the speech bubble?

Brain work

After you have tackled questions 1–4, think about the Brain work activity on page 57. Make some notes about what you would say about William at his funeral service. Some handy words might be:

- luck
- mistake
- patient
- commander
- terrorising

How did William the Conqueror secure his Norman empire?

Defending the conquest

William was now king of England, but how long would he last? There were about 10,000 Normans in England supporting him, but they were surrounded by a hostile population of one to two million English people. From 1067 to 1075 William spent most of his time in England putting down rebellions against his rule by English lords (thegns). Source 1 shows how widespread these rebellions were and that William also had enemies in France.

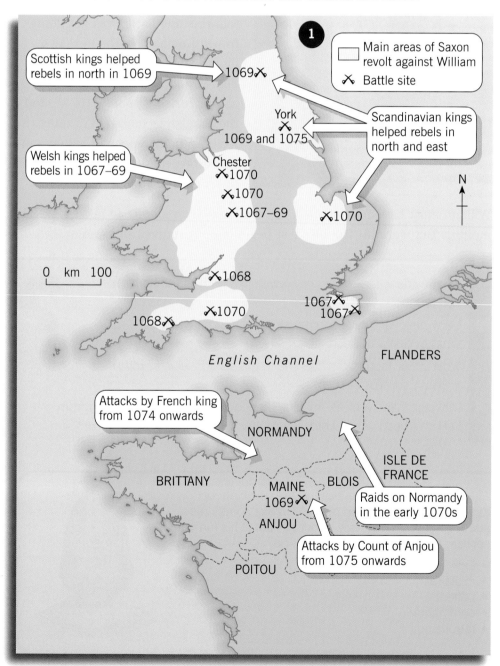

SOURCE 1 ◀
Threats to William, 1067–1075.

SOURCE 2 ▼
Part of a speech given by William while he was near to death in 1087. It was written down by the monk Ordericus Vitalis in about 1123.

❝ I attacked the English of the northern shires like a lion. I ordered their houses and corn, with all their implements and belongings, to be burnt without exception and large herds of cattle and beasts of burden to be destroyed wherever they were found. It was there that I took revenge on masses of people by subjecting them to a cruel famine; and by doing so – alas! – I became the murderer of many thousands, both young and old, from that fine race of people. ❞

The French king was afraid that being king of England would make William too powerful. He could be a threat to the French king. From around 1074 William faced attacks from the French king, Philip, the Count of Flanders and the Count of Anjou. So how did William overcome these threats?

The Harrying of the North

The most serious threat to William was the rebellion in the north of England in 1069. The northern English earls had joined with the king of Scotland and a Viking fleet of 250 ships. If they were not stopped, William would lose the whole of the north – and would it stop there?

William dealt with the rebellion ruthlessly. His actions became known as the Harrying of the North (see Source 3).

The population of the north fell dramatically. Southern England was flooded with terrified, starving refugees. William carried out the same policies in Staffordshire and Cheshire as well. The wealth of the north and much of the Midlands was destroyed. By about 1075 the Saxon thegns had all fled to Europe or Scotland. Their devastated lands did not have the people or resources to support a rebellion against William.

SOURCE 3 ▲

An artist's impression of the Harrying of the North.

1 Explain why William was so worried about the rebellion in the north.

2 Read Source 2 carefully. Describe William's actions as though you were talking to one of your friends.

3 William was close to death when he spoke the words in Source 2. Does this make the source more or less reliable as a source for the historian?

4 Do you think Source 3 is an accurate reconstruction? What evidence led you to this view?

After you have tackled questions 1–4, think about the Brain work activity on page 57. Make some notes about what you would say about William at his funeral service. Some handy words might be:

- rebellion
- north
- France
- ruthlessly
- Harrying of the North

Which other factors allowed William to keep his empire?

The Harrying of the North was a key reason why William survived the threats against him. It effectively wiped out the existing English lords in large parts of the country. However, we need to remember that William also overcame threats to his empire in Cheshire, the Midlands, the south west of England, Wales, Scotland and France! Several factors help to explain his success:

- **William was lucky** because the rebellions against him were not co-ordinated. This allowed him to defeat them one at a time.

- **William was able to do deals** with the Welsh, Scottish and Scandinavian kings who supported the rebels. He persuaded or bribed them to stop supporting the rebels.

- **William was a very effective military leader**. He took big risks, but he got away with them. For example, in 1069 he marched troops across northern England in winter. This took the rebels by surprise – medieval armies almost never marched in winter.

- **William and the Normans quickly developed a network of castles**. These provided bases which Norman troops could use to control areas once rebellions had been crushed (see Sources 4 and 5).

- **William appointed loyal barons he could rely on**. William placed his most loyal and able barons in the most important positions. After 1075 he spent most of his time fighting in France. In fact, he died fighting near Mantes in 1087. While he was in France he relied on men like Archbishop Lanfranc to run the government. He appointed marcher lords to defend him from Scottish and Welsh threats (see Source 4). These men were crucial to William's Norman empire. They allowed him to keep hold of his lands in England *and* in France at the same time.

SOURCE 4 ▼

Castles built in England during the reign of William the Conqueror.

The Bishop of Durham was given the same role in the north. His job was to stop any threat from Scotland.

The earls of Chester, Shrewsbury and Hereford were almost independent rulers known as 'marcher lords'. Their job was to make sure there was no threat to William from Wales.

SCOTLAND

Newcastle
Durham
York
Chester
Shrewsbury
WALES
Hereford
Canterbury
Dover

N

0   km   100

Marcher lords appointed by William
Castles

An artist's impression of Stafford Castle. Stafford was one of the areas which rebelled against William in 1070.

Brain work

How did William secure his Norman empire?

Luck	Loyal barons	Castles	William's skill as military leader	?	?

1 Make your own versions of these cards and write the heading for each card at the top. If you think some factors have been missed out, create new cards of your own.

2 On each card, write some examples of each of these factors and how they helped William secure his Norman empire.

3 Which factor do you think played the biggest part in William's success? Arrange the cards from top to bottom to show what you think was their order of importance in helping William secure his Norman empire.

4 After you have tackled this Brain work section, think about the Brain work activity on page 57. Make some notes about what you would say about William at his funeral service. Some handy words might be:

lucky • barons • castles • effective leader • deals

Who gained and lost in the Norman empire?

The Domesday Survey: Two places in Yorkshire, 1086

To try to answer the question at the top of this page, we are going to visit Yorkshire in 1086 with this band of travellers. They are travelling through Yorkshire to see what the land in the county is worth. At Christmas 1085 William ordered a detailed survey of his kingdom. Our monks, and hundreds of others like them, aim to give William a clear idea of what is going on in his English lands. Sources 1 and 2 show what our monks found in two places in Yorkshire (you can see the location of York in Source 4 on page 62). Remember this area was devastated in the Harrying of the North in 1069.

KEY WORDS

Burgess
Cathedral
Legal
Merchant
Petty burgess
Shilling
Smallholder
Society
Villager
Villein

1

The English lord who owned Wath before 1066.

A hide of land was the amount of land needed to support a family.

Ploughs were used to get the land ready for planting crops. The number of ploughs usually indicated how wealthy a village was.

Reitharr had 6 hides of taxable land with 3 ploughs. Roger de Bully now has 1 plough there; and 4 villeins and 8 smallholders with 1 plough. Value before 1066, 40 shillings; now 10 shillings.

The Norman knight who owned Wath in 1086.

Domesday Commissioners estimated the value of the land in 1066 and in 1086.

SOURCE 1 ◀
An extract from the Domesday Survey in Yorkshire for the village of Wath, near Pontefract.

An extract from the Domesday Survey for Ilkley, a village near York.

> Total of 66 hides taxable. English Archbishop Aldred had this in 1066 **2** with 35 ploughs. Now Archbishop Thomas of Bayeux has it with 2 ploughs; and 6 villeins and 10 smallholders have 10 ploughs. There are 5 freemen who have 4 villeins and 9 smallholders with 5 ploughs. A church and a priest with 1 villein and a plough. The largest part of this manor is waste. Value before 1066 £10; now £3.

Info point

The Domesday Survey

The survey spelled out what was owned by different groups in society.

- *In 1086 William wanted the information gathered by this survey so he could find out how rich the country was and who was wealthiest so he could raise taxes.*
- *Freemen were small farmers who rented their land from the local lord.*
- *Villeins were peasants who were given some land by the lord but spent much of their time working for him.*
- *Smallholders were poorer peasants who worked for the lord and looked after a small plot in their own time to feed their families.*
- *Burgesses were merchants.*
- *Petty burgesses were shopkeepers.*

Other sources about Yorkshire in 1086

Today, historians find records like these from the surveyor's notes useful for studying the impact of William's rule in Yorkshire. Other sources also help. For example, the accounts of Ilbert de Lacy, who owned the town of Pontefract, show that in 1086 he was building a stone castle. This created work for local craftsmen and business for the Pontefract shopkeepers. Some of Ilbert's contracts with his tenants show that villagers and smallholders had better lands in 1086 than they did in 1066. This was because William's Harrying of the North killed so many people. There was now plenty of good land to go around. Archbishop Thomas of Bayeux (see Source 2) owned Ilkley but spent more time in York than he did in the village. Thomas's accounts show he was building one of the many Norman cathedrals which we can still see all over England today. This brought jobs and economic recovery to areas around York, including Ilkley.

1 Read Sources 1 and 2 carefully. What do the sources tell you about what happened to the English lords who owned the land in 1066?

2 Imagine you are a historian trying to find out whether people were better or worse off under Norman rule. Explain how and why Sources 1 and 2 are useful to you.

3 Look back at your answer to question 2. Explain why having Sources 1 and 2 **and** the information about Ilbert de Lacy's and Thomas of Bayeux's accounts is helpful to the historian.

Brain work

After you have tackled questions 1–3, think about the Brain work activity on page 57. Make some notes about what you would say about William at his funeral service. Some handy words might be:

- Domesday Survey
- creating work
- land ownership
- land value
- ploughs.

Domesday 1086: The national picture

From studying Yorkshire in the last few pages, you have probably realised that William replaced all the English lords and bishops with Normans. You will also have seen that the north was in a pretty bad state after the Conquest. Most areas were worth less in 1086 than they were in 1066. On the other hand, there was economic recovery in some areas, like Pontefract and York.

Wulfric and Eda, Yorkshire smallholders

The people at the top

So, was this the national picture? The evidence we have does seem to present a similar picture:

- Domesday Book suggests that England was recovering from its troubles by 1086. The Domesday Survey valued the whole country at £73,000. This made it the richest country in northern Europe.

- Domesday Book tells us that in 1086 there were only four important English lords. We also know that after 1070 William appointed many new bishops in England. Not one was an Englishman.

- About 4000 English thegns lost their land. William gave their land to 200 loyal Norman barons. In return, these lords promised to make sure William's laws were obeyed. They also promised to provide William with troops when he went to war.

Eotheod, an English thegn from Cheshire

- The Norman lords (like Ilbert de Lacy in Pontefract) and bishops then divided their lands to reward their followers. Their followers were knights who fought in their armies. In return for land, they had to help the lord provide the troops that William needed for his armies.

- These knights then parcelled out lands to the freemen, villeins and smallholders.

The ordinary people

Domesday tells us a lot about the richest, most important people in society. It is not so easy to see what happened to slightly less important people under Norman rule. However, we do know about some people. For example, there was a priest in London called Regenbald. He drew up many legal documents for Edward the Confessor. He also drew up documents for William the Conqueror. This suggests that many of the ordinary officials in the government who did the day-to-day work kept their jobs after the Norman invasion.

Ilbert de Lacy, Norman lord of Pontefract

It is much more difficult to work out how the Conquest affected ordinary people in English villages. Most historians think that the Conquest did not affect them very much. Freemen, villeins and smallholders still worked their lands and their lord's lands. The only difference was that their lords were Normans after 1066 rather than Saxons.

Alfred, a freeman from Ilkley, and his wife, Helga

Edgar Wulstrun, a carpenter from York

Simon Fleming, a merchant

Some historians suggest that there is some evidence that ordinary people suffered under the Normans. The Normans introduced new forest laws. These laws meant that only the king and his lords could hunt deer in the forests. Peasants could no longer use this land as a source of food. There were harsh penalties for any English peasants caught hunting in the forests. On the other hand, law and order seems to have improved under the Normans. Peasants and merchants felt safer when they were taking their goods to market. They were less likely to be robbed.

4   In groups, write short character cards for each of the people shown here, listing the ways in which they may have gained or lost under Norman rule.

5   a Divide your classroom into three zones:
    • definite winners
    • not much change
    • definite losers.
    b Choose eight people in your group to represent each of the characters. Decide in which zone each person should sit.

6   In your original groups, discuss this question: 'Did the Norman Conquest create more winners than losers?'

Brain work

Think about the Brain work activity on page 57. Imagine you are the bishop again. You have to think about what you would say at William the Conqueror's funeral service.

1   Make a list of all the things you could possibly say about William.

2   Divide these things into categories:
    a Which things show that William was a great leader?
    b Which things show that he was just a lucky leader?
    c Which things show that he was a cruel and ruthless man?
    d Which things show that most people either prospered or did not suffer under William's rule?

3   Decide what you want to say about William. You need to remember two key things:
    a You will have to put a positive 'spin' on everything you say about William. If you mention the bad things he did, you must give the impression that he had good reasons for doing these things, or that he could not avoid doing them.
    b Aim to come up with about 250 words, and choose your words carefully.

Extension work
Look back at characters A–C on page 57. Imagine that the bishop and these three people meet up again at William's funeral feast. Plan a short role-play in which the characters discuss what the bishop said at the funeral.

How did William's Norman empire stand the test of time?

We have spent a lot of time looking at William's reign, so we are now going to fast-forward through about 130 years of history to see how the Norman empire that William created developed after his death. As you might expect, it is a story of high points and low points.

William II to Henry I

William the Conqueror had three sons: Robert, William Rufus and Henry. When he died, his empire was divided. Robert became Duke of Normandy. William Rufus became king of England. However, William Rufus died in 1100 in a hunting accident and his younger brother Henry quickly claimed the English crown, becoming Henry I of England. At the time, Robert was crusading in the Holy Land, but when he returned home he claimed the English throne from his younger brother. The two brothers went to war. Henry defeated Robert and recaptured Normandy in 1106. He had reunited his father's cross-Channel empire. Robert was imprisoned for life.

Stephen to Henry II

In 1120 Henry I's son drowned in a storm while crossing the English Channel. When Henry himself died in 1135, his daughter Matilda claimed the throne. However, so did Henry I's nephew, Stephen. The English barons supported Stephen at first, and crowned him king. However, Matilda and her husband, Count Geoffrey of Anjou, decided to fight for the throne. Many barons supported Matilda. The result was 20 years of terrible civil war. Law and order fell apart (see Source 1).

Eventually the two sides reached a compromise. Stephen kept the throne, but when he died the new king would be Matilda's son, Henry II. William the Conqueror's Norman empire now became the huge Angevin empire (see Source 2). Henry II was the most powerful ruler in Europe. He controlled even more French land than the French king! But he was not satisfied. In the 1160s he attacked Wales. In 1157 he took Northumbria back from the king of Scotland. From 1169 to 1172 Henry extended English rule to the south-east corner of Ireland.

Richard I and John

Henry II's eldest son was Richard. He ruled from 1189 to 1199 and spent very little of that time in England. He spent most of 1190 to 1194 crusading in the Holy Land. During that time, the French king captured a number of areas of Richard's lands in France.

KEY WORDS
Campaigning
Crusading
Holy Land

SOURCE 1 ▼
An extract from the Anglo Saxon Chronicle *commenting on the reign of Stephen. The* Chronicle *was written at the time of these events.*

❝ The barons filled the country full of castles and oppressed the wretched ① people. They levied taxes on the villages and called it protection money. When the wretched people had no more money, they robbed and burned so that you could easily go a whole day's journey and not find a village with anyone living in it. ❞

SOURCE 2 ▶
The empire of Henry II.

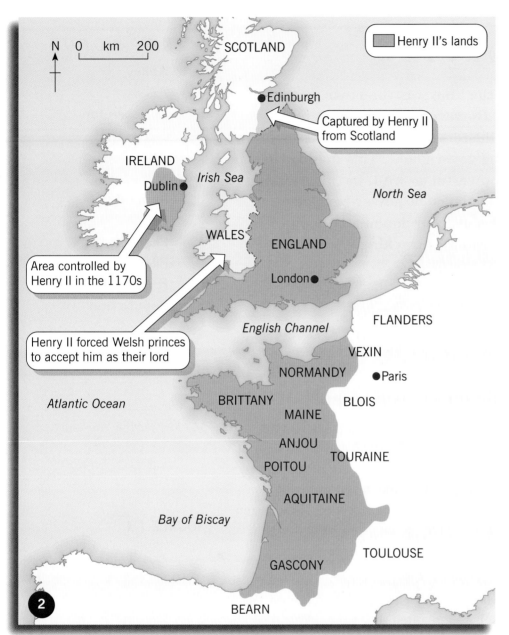

N 0 km 200

SCOTLAND

●Edinburgh

Captured by Henry II from Scotland

IRELAND

Irish Sea

Dublin●

North Sea

WALES

ENGLAND

London●

Area controlled by Henry II in the 1170s

Henry II forced Welsh princes to accept him as their lord

FLANDERS

English Channel

VEXIN

NORMANDY

●Paris

Atlantic Ocean

BRITTANY

BLOIS

MAINE

ANJOU

POITOU

TOURAINE

Bay of Biscay

AQUITAINE

TOULOUSE

GASCONY

2

BEARN

Henry II's lands

Much of the rest of Richard's reign was spent campaigning to get these lands back. After five years' more campaigning, Richard had retaken most of his lands. He was killed in France in 1199, having gained no new territories but without losing any either. Richard was followed by his brother, John. John was not as fortunate or as skilful as Richard in war. He was a strong ruler in England and was very effective at collecting taxes for his wars. Unfortunately for him, he was unsuccessful in those wars. Between 1200 and 1204 he lost Normandy, Brittany, Poitou and Aquitaine. He lost Gascony for a while but then reconquered it in 1206. On the other hand, John did extend England's power in Ireland. By 1215 he controlled about twice the amount of land in Ireland as Henry II had controlled.

Brain work

This section describes many ups and downs in the history of William's cross-Channel empire. Read through all the events and decide where you think they should go on this diagram. You may find it helpful to work in pairs.

High points				
1066	1100	1150	1200	1215
Low points				

OVERVIEW

In the medieval period the king was the most powerful person in the country. However, as time went on, he needed officials and ministers to help him make laws, collect taxes and run the government. This made other figures in the country powerful as well. In this section you will look at the balance of power between monarchs and the barons, churchmen and people who were ruled by the king.

KEY WORDS
Abbey
Abbot
Christendom
Cleric
Jew
Minister
Monastery
Nun
Pilgrim
Pilgrimage
Pope
Reputation
Tithe

Why was the medieval church so important?

How was the medieval church organised?

The medieval church was a very large international organisation. Medieval Christians called the area we call Europe today Christendom – the land of the Christians. Whether you were French, English, German or Italian, almost everyone during this period was a Christian. If you were not (for example, if you were a Jew) you were thought to be a second-class citizen. Many Jews were persecuted by Christians in the medieval period.

Clerics were definitely not second-class citizens. Clerics were churchmen – priests or bishops at the centre of religious and church life. There were also many lesser clerics, churchmen who could not carry out church services. Some of these men were students, but more often they were administrators or secretaries. Even so, these men still belonged to the Church.

The head of the Church was the Pope, who lived in Rome. He was the head of all the various branches of the Church in all the Christian countries. Below him were the archbishops and bishops. They controlled the Church's lands and appointed priests. They also ran the Church courts.

SOURCE 1 ◀

A government document recording the money collected in taxes from Dorset in 1130. You can see how important it was to have officials who could read and write.

SOURCE 2 ▼

Jews being beaten by a soldier. The Church did not allow Christians to lend money, so many Jews went into this trade.

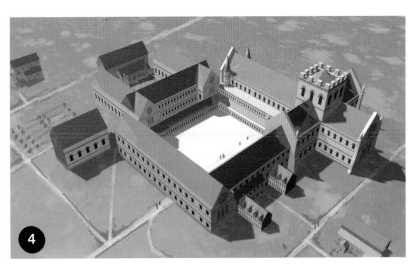

SOURCE 3 ▲

A bishop punishing a monk in a Church court. The monk is being forced to sit in the stocks.

SOURCE 4 ▶

A reconstruction drawing of a monastic community at Tupholme in Lincolnshire.

These courts were separate from the king's courts. If clerics did something wrong, they could only be tried in Church courts, not in courts where ordinary men and women were tried.

Another branch of the Church was the monasteries (often called abbeys). The monasteries were separate communities of monks (men) or nuns (women) who combined work and worship. They originally began as simple communities in remote areas. However, by the later medieval period the monasteries had grown. Many had large church buildings and huge lands. Abbots (the heads of monasteries) were often very rich and powerful people.

So, now you know a bit about how the Church was organised. But why was it so important? Turn the page to find out!

Brain work

Imagine you are working on a presentation, using ICT, on how the medieval Church was organised. You have put together a slide with the following bullet points:

- International organisation.
- Clerics.
- The Pope.
- Bishops and archbishops.
- Monasteries.

Your audience will see only the bullet points when you make your presentation. Write short notes to help you explain each of these bullet points to them.

Extension work

Prepare and make this presentation to the rest of your class. Try to really impress them by not using any notes at all. It's not as hard as you think. If you write good notes in the first place, you will remember the main points you need to include. You may be able to use some images in your presentation as well.

Reason 1: The Church was the link between heaven and earth

For many people, rich and poor, the most important thing in their life was to make sure they would go to heaven when they died. Kings tried to please God by building churches or giving land and money to the Church (see Source 5).

However, not many men or women were rich enough to give the Church land or expensive presents. They had to find other ways to give to the Church. For many people, their greatest ambition in life was to go on a pilgrimage – a visit to a holy place – so that they could show their commitment to the Church. Wealthy pilgrims might have gone to Rome to see the Pope. Others might have tried to visit Canterbury Cathedral (see Source 6). Wealthy people felt that gifts and pilgrimages increased their chances of going to heaven. Also, giving money and gifts to the Church gave people status in their local communities.

Even the poorest in society went to church regularly. In return, they got something from the Church. Many low-paid labourers worked on the building sites of the great cathedrals. They were not just doing their job. They were doing God's work. The poor peasant and his family might have a hard life, but if they went to church, prayed hard and gave what they could to the Church, there was a good chance they would go to heaven when they died.

Reason 2: The Church provided a living for men and women

The Domesday Book showed that in 1089 the Church owned about one quarter of the wealth of England. Some of its income came from tithes. All peasants had to pay a tithe – one tenth of their income to the Church every year. This paid for the upkeep of the parish church and the local priest. As the Church owned so much land, for a large number of ordinary men and women their landlord was the Church. So they paid rent and tithes to the Church. As well as rent, the Church made a lot of money from selling wool. This came from sheep reared on Church land.

Source 7 shows how a monastery like Furness Abbey in northern England was both an important religious centre and a thriving business community. Furness itself had many monks who lived a life which combined hard work and prayers. There was also a nunnery at Furness Abbey.

Finally, the local church was a place where you could get help. Churches and monasteries like Furness Abbey gave food and money to the poor. They also helped the sick.

SOURCE 5 ◀

An image of King Richard the Lionheart. He is shown with a church in his hand to show him as a protector and friend of the Church.

SOURCE 6 ◀

A party of wealthy pilgrims on the road to Canterbury in the late 1400s.

SOURCE 7 ▼

The business and religious interests of Furness Abbey around 1230.

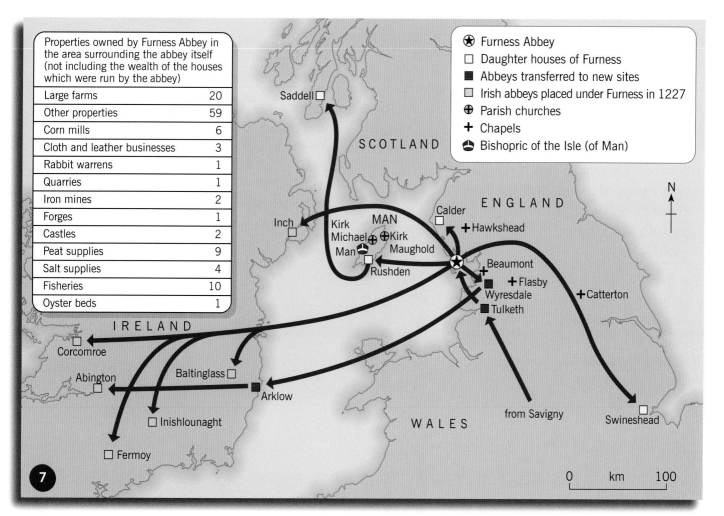

Properties owned by Furness Abbey in the area surrounding the abbey itself (not including the wealth of the houses which were run by the abbey)	
Large farms	20
Other properties	59
Corn mills	6
Cloth and leather businesses	3
Rabbit warrens	1
Quarries	1
Iron mines	2
Forges	1
Castles	2
Peat supplies	9
Salt supplies	4
Fisheries	10
Oyster beds	1

⊛ Furness Abbey
☐ Daughter houses of Furness
■ Abbeys transferred to new sites
☐ Irish abbeys placed under Furness in 1227
⊕ Parish churches
+ Chapels
⬥ Bishopric of the Isle (of Man)

SCOTLAND

ENGLAND

Saddell ☐

Inch ☐

Kirk Michael ⊕ MAN ⊕Kirk
Man ⬥ Maughold
Rushden ☐

Calder ☐
+Hawkshead

+Beaumont
■ +Flasby
Wyresdale
■Tulketh

+Catterton

IRELAND

Corcomroe ☐

Abington ☐

Baltinglass ☐

Arklow ■

☐ Inishlounaght

☐ Fermoy

WALES

from Savigny

Swineshead ☐

N

7

0   km   100

Reason 3: The Church ran the government

The Church was a very large organisation. There were thousands of churchmen (clerics). At the top were bishops, archbishops and abbots. They were important churchmen *and* great lords who ruled large amounts of land. Bishops and priests collected taxes for the king. They had their own law courts. Most clerics could read and write. They drew up documents, and took care of the king's accounts and other administration. Therefore, men of the Church had great influence over the government of the country.

Reason 4: The Church was powerful

The Church was so powerful it could even argue with the king. There were three really famous arguments between kings and the Church in the medieval period. One came in the reign of William Rufus (1087–1100). He argued with Anselm, the Archbishop of Canterbury. Anselm complained that Rufus was taking too much tax from the Church. He also complained about lay investiture. Lay investiture allowed kings to choose bishops. Most churchmen wanted the Pope, the head of the Church, to choose bishops. Eventually, a compromise was reached. The Pope chose bishops but he had to consult the king about who he chose.

In another case, King John (1199–1216) got into a major argument with the Pope. In 1205 the Pope wanted a man called Stephen Langton to be Archbishop of Canterbury. John disagreed and refused to accept Stephen. The Pope passed an interdict on England. The interdict meant that all church services stopped and no services like burials or marriages took place. Eventually, John gave in to the Pope and accepted Stephen Langton.

The most famous clash between the king and the Church came in the time of Henry II. The clash ended in the murder of Archbishop Thomas Becket in 1170. You are going to look at this clash in detail on pages 76 to 79.

SOURCE 8 ▼
A portrait of Archbishop Anselm from a manuscript produced in the late 1100s.

SOURCE 9 ▼
Pope Innocent III giving St Francis permission to start a new monastery.

Reason 5: The Church wrote the history books

You have already seen that the Church was important during this period in history because clerics could read and write. You have already come across written sources from several chronicles and history books that were written by monks. William the Conqueror gave a lot of money to the Church and built several churches and monasteries. Not surprisingly, most of the medieval history books were very favourable towards William. They were written by men who gained from the king's generosity!

SOURCE 10 ▼

A monk copying a book in the 1300s. There was no printing at this time, so books had to be copied by hand.

It is a very different story with kings like William II and John. Most of the history books are critical of these rulers because their relationships with the Church were not so good. Kings cared about their reputations, so they always thought twice before they argued with the Church.

Brain work

Imagine a local primary school has come to you for help. Its pupils are doing a study of a nearby church, which goes back to medieval times. They have found some records which show that many people gave money to the church or paid for parts of the building to be extended or repaired. Poor peasants did this as well as rich and powerful people. The pupils cannot understand why people did this. The school wants you to give the pupils a presentation about why people thought the Church was important.

Put together a presentation that explains all the reasons outlined on pages 72–75 and any more you can think of.

- You could organise your presentation around the five reasons on these pages.
- Your presentation should be in a similar bullet point format to the one you used in the Brain work activity on page 71.
- If you can, use some of the picture sources as well. It may be possible to use only these sources instead of bullet points to really capture the pupils' imagination.

How and why has the story of Becket changed?

You have already read about some of the clashes between kings and the Church in the medieval period. You are now going to look at the most famous clash. In 1162 Thomas Becket became Archbishop of Canterbury. Very soon he clashed with King Henry II over a number of issues. The arguments resulted in Becket's murder in 1170 in Canterbury Cathedral. The murder caused a sensation. It also made a reputation for Becket. In the medieval period everyone knew that he was a churchman cruelly murdered by supporters of a harsh king. The story grew and grew, and Becket became a saint. However, in the twentieth century the story seemed to change. In this section you are going to look at how the story has changed.

Brain work

1 How are the stories different? As you look through each of the accounts you should make a careful note of what each one says. You may find it helpful to draw up a table like the one below.

2 When you have completed your table, make a list of the main differences between the stories. These might include:

a different events covered.

b different sources or evidence used.

c different issues tackled (e.g. reasons for Becket's death as opposed to events of Becket's death).

d different impressions given of Henry II and Becket.

e other differences you have noticed.

Events in the story of Becket's death	How these events are described in...			
	1175 (Source 1)	1955 (Source 2)	1965 (Source 3)	2002 (Source 4)
Why Becket and Henry II clashed				
Actions of Henry II before Becket's death				
Actions of Becket before his death				
The murder of Becket				
Actions of Henry II after Becket's death				
Other features of the story which you think are important				

Keep your work in a safe place – you will need it for the next Brain work activity.

SOURCE 1 ▼

The story in about 1175 – an extract from an account of the murder of Becket by Edward Grim. Grim was a close friend of Becket and was present when he was murdered.

❛ When the holy archbishop Becket entered the church, the monks tried to bolt the doors of the church to protect the archbishop from his attackers. But the champion of good [Becket] stopped them, saying, 'It is not right to make a fortress of the house of prayer, the church of Christ.'

[Henry's knights then entered the church and argued with Becket. Then one of the knights struck Becket with his sword.]

Then he received a second blow on the head but still stood firm. At the third blow he fell on his knees, saying in a low voice, 'For the Name of Jesus and the protection of the Church I am ready to embrace death.' Then the third knight inflicted a terrible wound as he lay, and the crown which was large was separated from the head. ❜

SOURCE 2 ▶

The story in 1955 – an extract from a school textbook called British History in Strip Pictures.

HENRY II AND BECKET

After Stephen's death in 1154 Matilda's son became King Henry II. With the help of his friend and Chancellor, Thomas Becket, Henry restored royal authority over the barons. Then, to increase his power over the Church, he desired that Becket should become Archbishop of Canterbury.

1. Becket was doubtful, for he knew and said that he would serve the Church as faithfully as he had served the King. But Henry insisted.

2. As Archbishop, Becket kept his word and defied Henry even when charged with treason. After this Becket fled to France.

3. Back in England again, Becket remained loyal to the Church, and Henry in a fit of temper said: "Will no one rid me of this turbulent priest?"

4. Four knights took the King at his word. Leaving Henry in France they crossed to England, rode to Canterbury and murdered Becket on the altar steps of the Cathedral.

5. In token of remorse for his wicked words Henry allowed the monks to thrash him.

> Until he became Archbishop, Becket had been the chief adviser to the King, and the two had been inseparable friends, but when the King wanted all clergymen to be tried, for any offences they might have committed, in civil courts, not Church courts, Becket quarrelled with his King, because he refused to allow this. Henry banished him to France, though he allowed him to return again a few years later. When Henry heard of the welcome accorded to Becket on his return, he flew into a great rage and said: 'What a parcel of fools have I in my Court, that not one of them will avenge me of this one upstart priest.' Four knights then went to Canterbury and murdered the Archbishop at the altar of his own cathedral.
>
> Everyone was shocked and Henry not the least of them, for he had never meant such a thing to happen. To save himself in the eyes of the people he had to walk to Canterbury and submit to being flogged by each of the priests at Canterbury. What was even harder for Henry was that he was no longer in a position to make demands upon the Church and he had lost the battle with Becket. It may happily be said that Henry was on better terms with his next great adviser, Bishop Hugh of Lincoln. >

SOURCE 3 ◀

The story in 1965 – an extract from a school textbook called A Pageant of History.

(3)

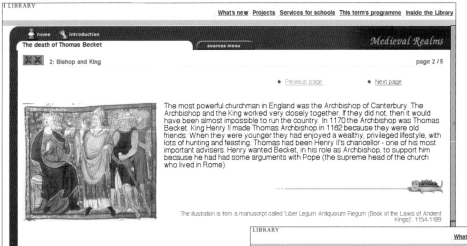

(4a)

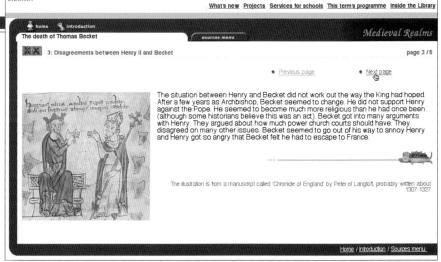

(4b)

SOURCE 4a–d ◀ ▶

The story in 2002 – sections 2–5 of a narrative of the story of Becket which was published on the British Library website.
© 2002 The British Library Board.
Web page design by Footmark Media Ltd. www.footmark.com

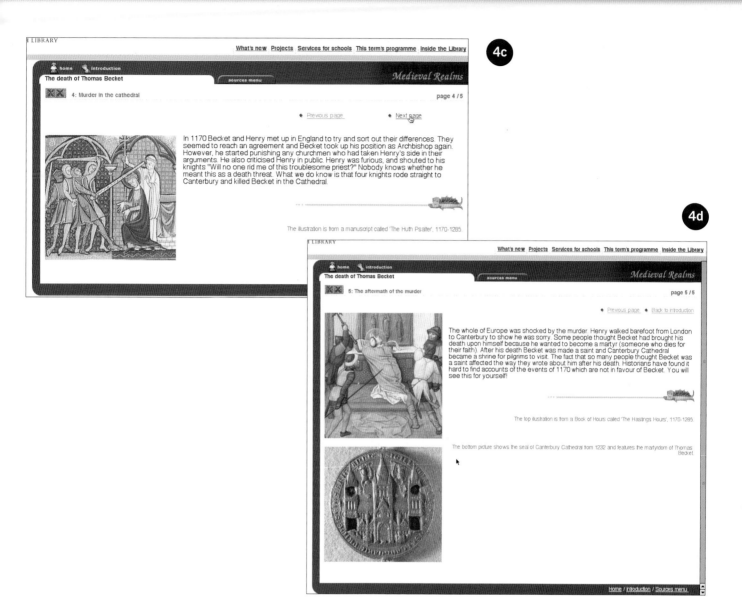

4: Murder in the cathedral

page 4 / 5

◆ Previous page   ◆ Next page

In 1170 Becket and Henry met up in England to try and sort out their differences. They seemed to reach an agreement and Becket took up his position as Archbishop again. However, he started punishing any churchmen who had taken Henry's side in their arguments. He also criticised Henry in public. Henry was furious, and shouted to his knights "Will no one rid me of this troublesome priest?" Nobody knows whether he meant this as a death threat. What we do know is that four knights rode straight to Canterbury and killed Becket in the Cathedral.

The illustration is from a manuscript called 'The Huth Psalter', 1170-1285.

5: The aftermath of the murder

page 5 / 5

◆ Previous page   ◆ Back to introduction

The whole of Europe was shocked by the murder. Henry walked barefoot from London to Canterbury to show he was sorry. Some people thought Becket had brought his death upon himself because he wanted to become a martyr (someone who dies for their faith). After his death Becket was made a saint and Canterbury Cathedral became a shrine for pilgrims to visit. The fact that so many people thought Becket was a saint affected the way they wrote about him after his death. Historians have found it hard to find accounts of the events of 1170 which are not in favour of Becket. You will see this for yourself!

The top illustration is from a Book of Hours called 'The Hastings Hours', 1170-1285.

The bottom picture shows the seal of Canterbury Cathedral from 1232 and features the martyrdom of Thomas Becket.

Home / Introduction / Sources menu

Brain work

Why are the stories different? Here are some of the possible reasons why the stories are different:

a The writers found different information.

b Only one of the writers actually saw what happened.

c The writers are biased one way or another.

d Different writers interpret the same sources and information differently.

e Writers select some events and leave others out, which changes the story.

f The writers were trying to tackle different issues.

Work in pairs or small groups.

1 Discuss each of these possible reasons and whether you think they explain the differences between Sources 1–4.

2 Decide which explanation you think is the best in this case, or come up with your own explanation for why they are different.

Why is Magna Carta still admired today?

> ❛ When representatives of the young republic of the United States gathered to draft a constitution [in 1776], they turned to the legal system they knew and admired – English law which evolved from Magna Carta. ❜ **1**

> ❛ I have always been a great believer in the Magna Carta and that justice delayed is justice denied. ❜ **2**

SOURCE 1 ◀

An extract from the website of the archives of the US government. It was part of a special exhibition on Magna Carta.

SOURCE 2 ◀

An English judge complaining about delays in the English legal system in 2002.

1 What does the writer of Source 1 admire about Magna Carta?

2 What does the writer of Source 2 admire?

Try using an Internet search engine and typing in 'Magna Carta' ('Magna Carta' is Latin for 'Great Charter'). You will turn up at least 50 websites about Magna Carta. Virtually all of them describe Magna Carta as a truly great document (see Source 1). Americans admire Magna Carta so much that American lawyers even built a special monument at Runnymede. That's the place where Magna Carta was signed in 1215. But does everyone think Magna Carta was great?

I don't understand why these people say Magna Carta was so great. It was simply a document that allowed a bunch of greedy barons to avoid paying taxes and push King John around to get their own way.

Historian A

Magna Carta was the start of a long process. Many of the points in Magna Carta were the foundations of the democratic rights we have today.

Historian B

KEY WORDS

Charter
Excommunicate
Fine
Inherit
Monument
Republic
Rights
Scutage

If we are going to understand this disagreement, we need to look at the events leading up to Magna Carta. We also need to look at Magna Carta itself.

The reign of King John

John has a reputation as a bad king, but this is probably a bit unfair. We have a lot of records from John's reign. These show that his government was very efficient. It was effective at collecting taxes. It got rid of a lot of corruption in government. John also faced many problems that his father Henry II and his brother Richard had not solved. Both Henry and Richard fought a lot of wars. Wars were expensive. Henry and Richard both tried new ways to get money out of the Church and the barons to pay for their wars. When John became king, he had wars too. The trouble was, by the time of his reign, the barons were fed up with being taxed.

On the other hand, we cannot ignore the major problems of John's reign. He was unsuccessful in three key areas.

1 War

John became king in 1199. Almost straight away, the French king Philip tried to take away his French lands. John went to war with Philip but was unsuccessful. By 1203 he had lost virtually all his lands in France. In 1213–1214 he tried again to get his French lands back, but he was defeated once more. The barons disliked paying tax anyway and they were very unhappy about paying taxes to fund wars that John lost.

2 Relations with the church

In 1205 John argued with the Pope about who should be the new Archbishop of Canterbury. The argument dragged on for eight years.

- During that time John confiscated lands belonging to the Church to raise money. When a bishop died, John stopped a new bishop being appointed. He kept the income from the bishop's land for himself.

- John also tried to intimidate any churchmen who supported the Pope instead of him.

- The Pope excommunicated John (threw him out of the Church). This worried John because it meant that anyone who rebelled against him would have the Church's support. Eventually, he had to give in. In 1213 he accepted Stephen Langton as archbishop.

3 Why did war make John's rule unpopular?

4 Why did John clash with the Church?

5 Did John come out on top in his clash with the Church?

3 Relations with the barons

John's relations with the leading barons in England were often very bad:

- He had a number of ministers who had put many of their relatives into good jobs. The barons disliked these ministers (and probably wanted some of the jobs they handed out for themselves).

- John brought in new royal courts of justice. This took power and influence away from the barons, who had run the courts.
- He was extremely suspicious. He used his courts to put several barons on trial for plotting against him. The royal courts were run by John's officials so they usually convicted the barons. Barons were usually tried by other barons (and often not convicted or given a light sentence).
- John needed money to pay for his wars. He found all kinds of ways of getting more money out of the barons. He charged the scutage tax almost every year. It was only supposed to be charged when England was at war. He also forced the barons to pay him large amounts of money when they inherited land. Other kings did this too, but John demanded much larger amounts of money. He charged some barons £6000 when they thought they should only pay about £100.
- Many barons simply did not support John. Some of them refused to serve him in his wars in France. He had to give up a plan to invade Wales in 1212 because some barons threatened to rebel against him. The man who led the revolt against him in 1215 was Robert Fitz Walter. He had a long-standing grudge against John.

6   Make a list of the reasons why John clashed with the barons.
7   Which reasons do you think upset the barons most?
8   Is it possible to say whether John or the barons were more to blame for the bad relations?

Magna Carta

The discontent with John came to a head in 1215. In January 1215 the barons asked John to stop measures like scutage but he ignored their demands. By May 1215 the barons had raised an army and were marching on London. In June, John was forced to accept their demands and sign Magna Carta. However, he quickly went back on his word and went to war against the barons again. So Magna Carta never really went into operation in John's reign.

From Magna Carta to the first Parliament

The civil war continued until John died in October 1216. His son, Henry III, was only a boy. A council of barons looked after the young king until he took control in 1232. Like his father, Henry was soon facing trouble from the barons. They were demanding that he should follow the terms of Magna Carta. Henry refused. This eventually led to another civil war. Henry had to accept control from a council of barons. This was the beginning of England's parliament (see the Info point).

So, was Magna Carta important or not? Now it's time to look closely at Magna Carta itself.

> 1 **The English Church shall be free for ever. The kings will not interfere with the rights of the Church.**
>
> 2 **In order to inherit land, a baron should pay £100, and a knight should pay 100 shillings.**
>
> 12 **The king will not charge scutage without consulting the wishes of the kingdom.**
>
> 14 **To obtain the consent of the kingdom to raise taxes, the king must consult his archbishops, bishops and barons.**
>
> 20 **If a freeman is fined for a crime, the fine should be related to the seriousness of the crime, not the king's need to raise money.**
>
> 21 **Barons may only be put on trial by their peers [other barons]. If they are found guilty, the fine should be decided by their peers.**
>
> 39 **No freeman can be arrested or outlawed without a fair trial.**

Info point

Parliament

- John's son was King Henry III. Like his father, Henry III clashed with the barons over Magna Carta.
- In 1258 the barons forced him to rule with the advice of a Great Council of barons.
- Henry soon quarrelled with the barons.
- This led to civil war. The barons were led by Simon de Montfort. In 1264 Simon defeated Henry in battle. He forced Henry to accept a new type of Great Council. This council included rich merchants and farmers as well as the great lords and bishops.
- Simon was killed in 1265. However, his idea of a Great Council lived on. In 1295 England had a new king, Edward I. He needed money to fight wars. He called a Great Council to agree on how to raise the money without causing another civil war.
- By this time the Great Council was known as parliament (which meant 'a place to talk'). The people who came to parliament represented their towns, counties, etc. They became known as Members of Parliament.

SOURCE 3 ◀

Extracts from Magna Carta. The full document had 63 sections, but we have just chosen a few. Remember that freemen meant people like merchants in towns or farmers on small farms. It did not include the vast majority of ordinary peasants.

SOURCE 3 (continued) ▶

Historian A

40 Any person arrested or put on trial must be tried as quickly as possible.

45 The king will only appoint officials who know the law of the land well and will observe it properly.

50 Gerard de Athee and all his family should be removed from their posts as royal officials and sent out of the country.

61 The king will agree to consult with a council of 25 barons to make sure that he rules in accordance with this charter.

63 The king confirms that the English Church will be free and that all the rights in this charter will be observed for ever. **"**

I don't understand why these people say Magna Carta was so great. It was simply a document that allowed a bunch of greedy barons to avoid paying taxes and push King John around to get their own way.

Historian B

Magna Carta was the start of a long process. Many of the points in Magna Carta were the foundations of the democratic rights we have today.

Brain work

Look through the terms of Magna Carta set out in Source 3. Think about historians A and B. Do the terms support the view of historian A or historian B? You could use a table like this to help you.

Terms of Magna Carta which support historian A	Terms which are not clear or could support either historian	Terms of Magna Carta which support historian B

Once you have completed your table, decide whether you agree with historian A or historian B.

OVERVIEW

In this section we are going to look at the period 1300–1500. We are also going to concentrate more on the lives of ordinary people. In many ways, people's lives did not change much in the medieval period. On the other hand, factors like war, disease and trade all had an impact on medieval towns and villages and the people who lived in them.

KEY WORDS
Demesne
Parson
Warp
Weaver

Why did some medieval people end up in court?

Historians find it relatively easy to find out about the lives of powerful people like kings, bishops and barons because there are lots of records that were written about them and lots of painting of them. However, it is much more difficult to find out about the lives of ordinary people. One of the best sources historians have are records of the many court cases involving medieval people.

Most medieval people who went to court ended up in the local manor court. The manor was the land owned by the local lord. It included the lord's own land and the land that he rented out to the people of the manor. The magistrate of the manor court was usually the local lord himself. There were also courts which dealt with cases in towns. They worked in a similar way.

The cases heard in the manor courts were not serious crimes like murders or robberies. These crimes were dealt with in the royal courts. Records of local court cases give historians a fascinating insight into what medieval people got up to, and how far they were able to get away with things!

Brain work

Why did some medieval people end up in court? Your task is to decide whether or not the following stories are true or made-up medieval court cases.

A   A parson once complained that his neighbours had built two large windows and could see everything that his tenants and servants were getting up to.

B   A villein was fined because he did not give his lord a chicken.

C   The king gave his pet ostrich to two men to raise some money by showing it off around the country and charging people to see it. In one town the men were mugged and the ostrich had its feathers plucked.

D   In one court case a neighbour complained about another neighbour because his sewage was soaking through the neighbour's walls.

E   Merchants who exported wool to Europe had to take it through the port of Calais. At Calais the king's officials charged tax on it. Some merchants tried to avoid paying taxes on their wool by going to a pub in Rotterdam called Calais. They could then say that they had taken their wool to Calais.

F   Some peasants were fined because they did not clean out their lord's ditch.

G   A group of weavers went to court to stop other weavers making cloth with stripes in it.

H   The job of guilds was to make sure that their members produced quality goods. One weaver was thrown out of the weaver's guild because he cheated his customers.

I   A young woman was made a ward of court because she got married without her lord's permission.

1 Before you look at Sources 1–6 on pages 88 and 89, decide which cases you think are probably real and which ones are made up.
2 Read through Sources 1–6 and see if you were right.

Extension work
After you have studied Sources 1–6, see if you can find other cases or judgements (true ones!) that are not on the list.

‘ Roger Aldith, John's son, was charged that he had twice offended against the rules of the gild: he had made a blanket which was partly of good warp thread [the up and down thread of a cloth] and partly of bad warp thread. He had his membership of the gild taken away and was expelled from the gild. ’

SOURCE 1 ◀

A decision from a guild of clothmakers in King's Lynn, Norfolk, in 1258.

‘ Matilda Coppelowe, Richard Qualm and Nocholas Kembald were each fined because they did not clean out the ditch above the demesne [the lord's land] as they promised the hayward [the official who looked after the fences on the manor] they would.

William Kembald the younger was fined 12d for keeping from his lord a hen for the last two years.

Alice the daughter of Robert Rede is to be placed under the control of the court because she married without permission from the lord of the manor.

John Green must return to the court at another time to answer to the lord for allowing his pigs to damage the fences in the meadow.

William Hawys was fined 18s for demolishing a house on his land without the permission of the lord. The lord agreed that it should not be rebuilt because nobody dares live there because of thieves.

The lord confirmed that William Patel, Nicolad Denys, Walter Qualm, Agnes and Alice Typetrot and Agnes Gooch should all be allowed to inherit their lands without paying a fee to the lord, because that is the custom in this manor [peasants usually had to pay a fee to inherit their lands]. ’

SOURCE 2 ◀

Judgements made at the local manor court of Walsham in 1329. Walsham is a village in Suffolk.

‘ William de Stanesfeld, parson of St Stephen de Walbrok, complains that Geoffrey Aleyn and Maud his wife have two newly made windows less than 16ft from the ground opposite their house through which their tenants can see all the private affairs of the William's tenants and servants; and that because Geoffrey and Maud do not have a gutter, their rainwater falls upon the parson's land; and, further, that they have two latrines [toilets] so closely adjoining Stephen's land property that the sewage penetrates and rots their timber and walls.

Having viewed the premises, the mayor and aldermen adjudge that, as far as concerns the two windows, there is not a valid complaint, but that within 40 days Geoffrey and Maud must build a stone wall 2ft thick or an earthen wall 3–4ft thick between their two latrines and the parson's property and repair their gutters. ’

SOURCE 3 ◀

An extract from the London Assizes (Courts) of Nuisance, 1341.

SOURCE 4 ▶

An extract from a court case brought in York in 1399.

❝ The weavers of the city of York pointed out that King Henry III [1216–1272] granted that nobody should make dyed or striped cloth in the county of Yorkshire except them; now many foreign weavers have often made such cloth and still continue to do so, in contempt of the king, and damaging the business of the weavers of York. ❞

4

SOURCE 5 ▶

Extracts from an enquiry by royal officials into the wool trade in 1366.

❝ John Kervyng of Rotterdam said three merchants had taken loads of wool to Rotterdam. There was, he said, a tavern in Rotterdam called 'Calais', and several others called 'France', 'England', 'Hemelrik', 'Helle'. And he said that when any merchants were in the tavern called 'Calais' and sold goods they said between themselves 'now we have been in Calais'. ❞

5

SOURCE 6 ▶

A lawsuit put before a court in Bury St Edmunds, Suffolk, in 1431.

❝ John Coyn of Bury in Suffolk and John Shepherd and John Goodbody of the same town on November 14th last at Bury assaulted Axsmyth and Piers, the keepers to whom the king had trusted his ostrich. They imprisoned them for five days, and arrested and plucked the ostrich grievously, and openly showed him for nothing to all manner of people. ❞

6

Brain work

We hope you have enjoyed reading about these court cases. But have you thought about why they are useful to historians?

1 In small groups, read the sources again and discuss what these court cases tell you about:

   a what peasants had to do for their lord.

   b what peasants needed their lord's permission to do.

   c the rights of peasants to inherit land.

   d the power of guilds.

   e international trade.

   f entertainment.

   g sanitation in medieval towns.

2 These court cases give you only a small glimpse of medieval life. Choose one topic from the list above and think about:

   a the questions you would like to ask about this topic.

   b the evidence which might help you answer your questions.

Would you rather live in the 1300s or the 1400s?

In recent years there have been a number of TV programmes in which present-day people pretend to live in an earlier time. We have seen *The 1900 House*, *The 1940s House*, *The Trench* and many others. These programmes claim to send people back in time. Let's imagine for a moment that you really could go back and live in another time. Where would you go and who would you be?

KEY WORDS

Archaeological
Bushel
Carding
Enclosed
Harvest
Plague
Psalter
Reconstruction
Spinning
Strip
Thatched roof
Weaving

Unfortunately, your time machine is a bit limited. You will have to go back as a medieval peasant and you have only two time zones to choose from – around 1300 or around 1400. Which would you choose? The next few pages will help you.

As you read through pages 90–101, keep careful notes of what life was like at each time. A table like this will help.

Brain work

Big issues	The situation in 1300	The situation in 1400
Where would I live?		
Who would I work for?		
What work would I do?		
Would I be free?		
What would I eat?		
What about my family?		
Would I travel much?		
Would I have good prospects?		

When you have finished time travelling, you will decide between 1300 and 1400 and list at least five reasons why you made your choice.

A peasant's life in 1300

Where would you live?

As a medieval peasant in 1300, you live in a small medieval village. Well over 90 per cent of the population of medieval Britain are peasants. By 1300 most live in small villages. The two most important buildings in the village are the lord's manor house and the church. Source 1 gives you an idea of what your village looks like.

SOURCE 1 ▼

A reconstruction of a medieval village in about 1300.

Each of the cottages in the village has a small garden where people keep a few chickens and a pig and grow some vegetables. The much larger fields around the village are divided into strips. The lord and the priest have the largest number of strips, and the peasants the least. By twenty-first century standards, even the poorest villein has a lot of land. On the other hand, the land does not produce anything like as much food as land farmed today using modern farming methods.

The top priority of everyone in the village is to grow as much food as possible, especially wheat. One crop is grown in each large field and this is changed each year. This is called crop rotation, which allows the fields to recover their minerals and nutrients (see Source 2).

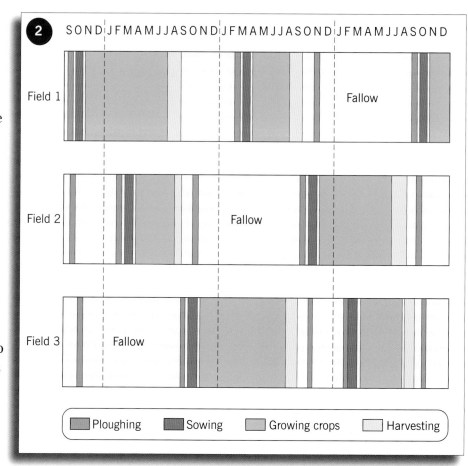

Ploughing   Sowing   Growing crops   Harvesting

1 Imagine you were flying over the village in Source 1 in a helicopter. Briefly describe what you can see, remembering that you are using a radio and the person at the other end of the radio cannot see the village.

2 a How was the land divided up in 1300?

b What was the thinking behind this division?

SOURCE 2 ▲

The rotation of crops in the three fields of a typical medieval village in central England. In some parts of the country animals were more important because wheat would not grow on high ground or very wet areas.

You live in one of the small cottages. In Source 1 the cottages are made of stone but medieval people prefer wooden houses. However, as the population grows the wood is starting to run out. Also, some areas do not have much wood. So, if you live in Kent, for example, you would probably live in a stone cottage like the one in Source 3. You live at one end of the building while your animals live at the other end.

Source 4 gives you an idea of the inside of a typical cottage, wooden or stone. The big advantage of stone cottages is that they are more fireproof. The combination of thatched roofs, wooden houses and open fires means that fire is a major hazard in medieval times.

SOURCE 3 ▶

A photograph of a reconstructed medieval cottage from the village of Hangleton in Sussex. The house was about 14 metres long and 5 metres wide.

SOURCE 4 ▶

A reconstruction drawing of the inside of a medieval cottage.

SOURCE 5 ▼

A list of possessions of William Lene, a villein from Walsham in Suffolk. William was killed in a fire in his barn in 1329. This record lists his belongings.

‘
- 3 large brass pots; 2 brass pans; basin and jug; table with 3 benches and 1 chair.
- 2 oxen; 8 cows; 1 bull; 3 calves; 1 mare and 1 foal; 30 sheep; 1 sow and 4 piglets.
- Granary containing wheat, rye, barley, beans, peas, oats, malt.
- 7s 8d in money.
- 3 wooden barrels; 4 vats; 2 tubs.
- 1 plough; 1 cart with unshod wheels.
- 3 geese; 1 cockerel; 6 hens.
- 10 yards of red cloth; 1 griddle; 2 straw baskets; 2 troughs; 1 robe for William's body; 4 linen sheets; 2 table cloths; 2 towels; 1 mortar and pestle.
- 12 acres of land sown with wheat. ’

---

3 Get back on the radio and describe the peasant's house.
Think about the sounds and smells as well as what you can see.

4 Do you think that William Lene (Source 5) was better or worse off than the villein who lived in the cottage in Source 4?
Explain your answer.

Who would you work for? What work would you do? Would you be free?

These questions are very closely linked. As a medieval peasant, you work for your lord. Most of your life is spent working in the fields on your land or on the lord's land. As a peasant, you might be either a villein or a freeman (see the Info point). Source 6 is a typical contract for a villein in about 1300.

> • **Richard Est will pay his lord one quarter of wheat in October. In November he will pay wheat, four bushels of oats and three hens. And at Christmas one cock and two hens and two pennies worth of bread.**
>
> • **He will work one day every week ploughing his lord's land.**
>
> • **And he will work a second day a week mowing or reaping, or whatever other work shall be imposed on him by the lord or his bailiff [this could involve digging or clearing ditches, mending fences, shearing sheep, keeping weeds out of ponds where fish were kept].**
>
> • **At harvest time he shall work two extra days and on each of those days he works he shall find two other men to work with him at his own expense.**
>
> • **Without his lord's permission he will neither marry his son or daughter [to someone else], nor sell his oxen or calves, nor his horses, neither will he fell the oak or ash trees without permission from his lord.**
>
> • **However often he brews he will give one penny to the lord.**

SOURCE 6 ◄

An agreement between a lord and a villein in Oxford in 1298.

A typical freeman rents his land from the lord. He lives in a similar house to the villein. However, it is larger. He may well have his animals outside in barns or outbuildings. He does not have to do week work (see the Info point) as long as he pays his rent. However, he might have to do boon (harvest) work. Lords have other ways of getting money out of their tenants as well. Freemen's wives have to get their corn ground into flour in the lord's flour mill. They also have to bake their bread in the lord's ovens. Of course, there is a charge for this. Like the villein, he pays tax on his beer. Freemen do not have the same restrictions as villeins on marriage and selling animals.

---

5 Make a list of the main duties that a villein had to carry out.

6 Make another list of the restrictions on the villein.

7 Look back to your work on the court cases on pages 88 and 89. Are there any restrictions which Richard Est does not have in his agreement?

Info point

Medieval peasants and their work

- *There were different types of medieval peasants.*

- *Serfs were at the bottom of society. They were a bit better off than slaves, but not much. They had to work the land for their lord. They could not leave the manor without the lord's permission.*

- *Villeins were the most numerous type of peasant. About 75% of peasants were villeins. The villein had a small farm or plot from the lord. In return, he did work on the lord's land. This was often known as week work.*

- *Week work was called this because villeins had to do a certain number of days' work per week for the lord.*

- *Freemen were better off than villeins. They made up about 25% of the population. Freemen rented land from the lord and paid rent. The freeman did not have to do week work but might have to do boon work.*

- *Boon work involved a certain number of days' work for the lord. It was usually at busy times like harvest.*

An image from the early 1300s showing peasants harvesting wheat. They are being ordered around by the lord's bailiff (his key official).

What would you eat?

Basically, you eat what you can grow. The typical diet for a peasant contains a lot of bread and cheese because the peasant can make his own. However, there is fish, eggs and a range of vegetables. There are no potatoes though – they did not come to England for another couple of centuries. Peasants mostly drink weak beer. They brew their own beer because it is not safe to drink the water. Meat is a special treat because animals are valuable and because meat does not keep. It can be smoked or salted to make it keep longer, but salt is expensive. Smoked bacon was probably the most common meat dish because pigs were easy to keep. The bad news for time travellers is that the only sweet taste you would get in 1300 is honey. The good news is that medieval teeth are generally in better condition than our teeth today! On a serious note, remember that famine is always a threat to the medieval peasant. In a bad year you could starve.

SOURCE 8 ▲
A medieval picture of ploughing in the early 1300s. This image does not give a real sense of how hard the job of ploughing was. The man in the centre is sowing seeds.

Brain work

1 Decide what kind of peasant you might be in 1300 and what kind of house you would live in. Add this information to the table you created for the Brain work activity on page 90.

2 Make a list of what you might eat in 1300. Add this information to the table you created for the Brain work activity on page 90.

What about your family?

Medieval people marry quite young – younger than most people marry in the twenty-first century. Apart from anything else, they cannot expect to live very long. The best life expectancy for a peasant is about 40 years. Being a medieval peasant is a hard and sometimes dangerous life. Not many people can survive without their families. Deaths are common from accidents, diseases and sometimes war.

If a peasant loses a husband or wife, they usually remarry quickly. Very often the lord orders a man or woman to remarry because families produce more work than single people. Church records show that many peasants marry several times in their lives.

SOURCE 9 ▲

A picture from a Bible published in about 1320 showing men's work and women's work. The men are breaking up the earth and planting seeds. The women are carding (combing) wool to get the fibres straight and spinning.

SOURCE 10a–c ◀

Scenes from the Luttrell Psalter (a prayer book) showing men and women working the land.

8	Was the medieval diet healthier than our diet today?
9	Explain why medieval people often married several times.
10	In what ways do Sources 9 and 10 give different views of the role of women?
11	Why were children important?

SOURCE 11 ▼

An extract from the court records of the manor of Stoke Prior in the Midlands, dated 1296.

❝ Simon Godith surrenders his land to his son in return for a room, a garden, a bakehouse, 5 butts of land in one croft and 4½ butts in Pertons Field. Simon's son will also pay him 8d a year and a cartload of sea-coal. ❞ **11**

SOURCE 12 ▼

A graph showing population and wheat prices in around 1300. There is no data for prices before 1200.

The family is a close-knit team that needs to work well together. The man of the family spends most of his time working on his own land or on the lord's land. This is often heavy work like harvesting wheat, pulling up weeds or breaking up hard clods of earth. Women and children usually have responsibility for the animals. Cows have to milked twice a day. Eggs have to be collected. Pigs have to be fed. Women also do domestic chores. Archaeological evidence suggests that cottages are regularly swept clean. Women also spend a lot of time carding, spinning and weaving cloth (mainly wool). All the evidence suggests that women are key players in the family team (see Sources 9 and 10).

Of course, we must not forget that women also bring up and look after the children on top of everything else! At busy times like harvest they may give the children to relatives to look after. Children are a vital part of the workforce, especially as they start to grow up. They work the land from an early age. They also look after elderly relatives. Many villeins inherit their land from their fathers while their fathers are still alive. In return, the villeins build their parents a small house on the land (see Source 11).

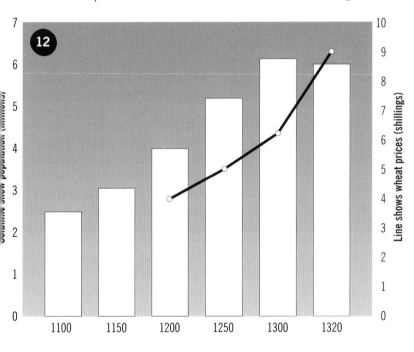

Would you have good prospects?

In 1300, the short answer is no. Britain's population has been rising steadily for a long time. Basically there is not enough land to go around. Any peasant who tries to get a better deal from his lord, for example by trying to do less week work, is likely to be thrown off his land. The lord can easily find someone else to take his place. Food prices are high (see Source 12). In fact, the price of most things is high compared to wages, which are low. Things in 1300 might sound bad, but that's nothing compared to how bad they are going to get.

Brain work

1 Decide what your family would be like in 1300 and what each member of the family would do. Add this information to the table you created for the Brain work activity on page 90.

2 You have reached the end of the 1300 section. Make sure you fill in the last rows in the table you have been working on.

A peasant's life in 1400

Welcome to 1400. In many ways, the life of the average villein or freeman has not changed much. The vast majority of them still work on the land. They still work the land for their lords. However, there are some important differences. To begin with, the village you live in now looks like the one in Source 13.

You are one of the lucky ones! For many people, their village now looks like the one in Source 14.

SOURCE 13 ◀

A reconstruction of a medieval village in about 1400.

SOURCE 14 ▼

A modern air photograph of the village of High Worsall in North Yorkshire. It was deserted by its people in the late 1300s. Many villages were deserted in the late 1300s and early 1400s.

Compare the 1400 village with the 1300 village. The fields are not as large in 1400. Some of the fields have been fenced off (enclosed) to keep in flocks of sheep. There are a lot more sheep than in 1300.

The strips owned by the villeins and the freemen are larger. So are their gardens and their houses. Even the poorer villeins have outbuildings to keep their animals in. In 1400 the villeins have more pots, jugs and similar items. A freeman's house is even more comfortable. There might even be the odd luxury, like some nice cloth or perhaps some sugar. Working conditions for villeins have improved.

12   Make a list of all the differences you can see between the village in Source 13 and the village in Source 1 on page 91.

13   Imagine you are briefing the artist who drew Source 4 on page 93 to draw an updated peasant house. What instructions would you give?

14   Read Source 15. Have conditions for peasants improved since 1300? (Hint: Look back at Source 6 on page 94).

SOURCE 15 ▶

An agreement between the lord and his tenants in Warkington, Lancashire, in 1386.

❝
- **Stephen Walker of Keteryng shall render to the lord 18 shillings yearly in four.**
- **He shall do two ploughings a year and will receive fair warning from the bailiff of when he will be needed.**
- **He shall still do week work, except that the lord will find him food and drink.**
- **At harvest time he shall reap for two days a week. On one day he shall find one man to work with him, on the second day he shall find two men. The men will be supplied with food by the lord.**
- **He shall give 4d to the lord for a horse if he decides to sell it.**
- **He shall pay a fine if he decides to marry his daughters [to someone else] and he shall pay the lord for his sons to attend school.** ❞

15

Peasants are still ploughing, digging ditches and harvesting. The work is just as hard. However, the peasants are a little better fed. Most houses have some meat in them. Families are smaller. There are not many children. Many more houses have one person in them. There are a lot of single women. They are mostly widows who have not remarried. Very few families have grown-up children living with their parents in the way we saw in 1300.

If you could talk to the peasants, you would find there are more who come from a long way away. They were not born in the village where they work. The villein in Source 15 is from Kettering in the Midlands. So why is he signing a contract in Lancashire? It is a sign of the good prospects most peasants have. These days the villeins can move around much more easily.

Lords compete with each other to give good terms to villeins. Many villeins have moved into the towns where wages are higher than in the countryside. Even the lords are doing quite well. When they started enclosing land to put sheep on, people complained that the lords valued the sheep more. The truth is that the lords just could not find enough peasants, which is why so many villages have died. Now the lords are making money from the wool merchants (see pages 102–105).

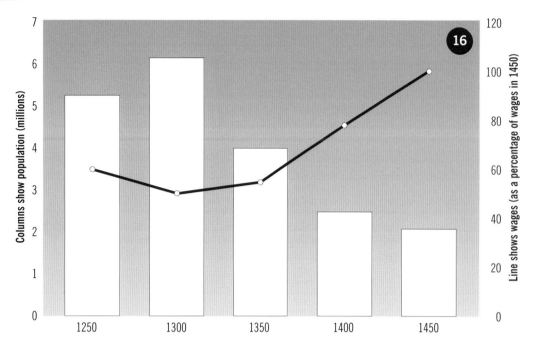

SOURCE 16 ◀

A graph showing population and wages after 1300.

Why are conditions in 1400 so different?

By this stage you are probably thinking that you definitely want to live in 1400. But let's consider what caused these changes. One of the main reasons why people are better off in 1400 is that there are far fewer of them (compare the population figures in Sources 12 and 16). As a result, the lords had to offer good conditions to get villeins to farm their land.

SOURCE 17 ▼

Mass burials of plague victims. This picture shows burials in the Netherlands, but similar scenes would have taken place in England.

The reason why there are so few people is plague, also called the Black Death. The plague arrived in July 1348. It swept across Asia and Europe and then it devastated Britain and Ireland. Some estimates suggest that half the population of Europe died in the great epidemic of 1348–1349. And, just as important, plague kept coming back! There were major national plagues in 1360, 1369 and 1375. There were many more local outbreaks every few years. This is why there are so many widows who have not married again. It is also why young adults do not live with their parents.

Before the plague, there were more peasants than were needed to work the land. So, a young adult would have to live with his parents until a farm became available or, more likely, he inherited the family farm. After the plague, there are many unoccupied farms so, at quite a young age, a peasant can become master of his own farm. By around 1400 the peasants are better off, but they pay a big price for this prosperity.

Brain work

1 Look at the information on pages 98–101 and fill in the second column of the table you created for the Brain work activity on page 90. Remember you are trying to list changes and differences.

2 Decide whether you would rather be a peasant in 1300 or 1400. Don't forget your list of at least five reasons why you chose 1300 or 1400.

Extension work

Imagine your history teacher has volunteered for a TV programme called *The Medieval House*. Your teacher and his or her family will live in a reconstructed medieval house and try to recreate the lives of medieval peasants.

The TV company that is making the series is called MadHistory Films Ltd. They want you to get your teacher ready for this experience. You will need to work in small groups and carry out two important tasks.

Task 1: Sit your teacher down in front of your group and explain:

• what life in 1300 was like.
• how life in 1400 was different from 1300 and why.
• what things you think your teacher will find the hardest.
  Make sure you find out whether they agree with you.

Task 2: Advise the TV company whether *The Medieval House* should be set in 1300 or 1400. You will have to explain:

• the main differences between 1300 and 1400.
• how far you can make a realistic reconstruction of life in 1300.
• how far you can make a realistic reconstruction of life in 1400.

You could turn all this work into a presentation for the teacher and the TV company, or you could create a large classroom display on the medieval house.

Why were there so many sheep in medieval England?

The story of Thomas Betson

We are going to start this investigation by looking at the life and work of Thomas Betson. He was a merchant of the Staple (see the Info point). This meant he was a very successful wool merchant.

If he was alive today he would be an international businessman, flying all over the world doing important deals.

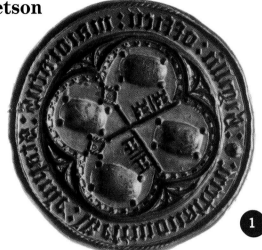

KEY WORDS
Dyeing
Woolsack

SOURCE 1 ◀

The mould used by the Mayor of the Staple to make seals in 1393. Seals were very important because they were used to show that documents were genuine.

1. Look at Source 1. Why is the writing on the mould backwards?
2. There are two types of objects on the mould. The keys represent St Peter, who looks after the gates of heaven. What is the other object and what does it represent?
3. The seal mould is solid silver. What does that suggest about the Staple?

We know a lot about Thomas Betson because he had a partner, Sir William Stonor. Thomas, William and their families wrote hundreds of letters to each other. We can find out a lot about the wool trade from these letters.

Thomas's business year began in the spring. Every year he got on his horse and rode off to the Cotswolds. He loved this journey. Some of his colleagues in the Staple travelled north to get wool. They bought it from the great abbeys like Fountains Abbey in Yorkshire, which owned enormous lands. Thomas thought that Cotswold wool was better. Anyway, he had many friends among the farmers and wool merchants in the Cotswold market town of Northleach. As soon as he arrived there he would stop at the church to thank God for his safe arrival. Then he would meet his friends in an ale house.

Info point

The Wool Staple

- The Wool Staple was a brilliant idea which involved co-operation between rulers and merchants in England and Europe.
- English merchants wanted to sell wool to Europe.
- Monarchs wanted to tax the wool exports.
- To make it easier for everyone, they formed an organisation called the Wool Staple. All the merchants agreed to buy and sell the wool in one place. This became the Staple town.
- For most of the medieval period, the Staple town was Calais in northern France. The wool merchants brought their wool to Calais.
- The Mayor (boss) of the Staple counted the bales of wool, collected the taxes from the merchants, gave the tax money to the monarch and allowed the merchants to sell their wool in Europe.

SOURCE 2 ▶
Brasses of a wool-man, his wife and 4 children, from the church at Northleach in the Cotswolds. Brasses were a kind of monument.

SOURCE 3 ▼
Medieval ships crossing the English Channel. These ships were ideal for transporting wool, which took up a lot of space but was not very heavy.

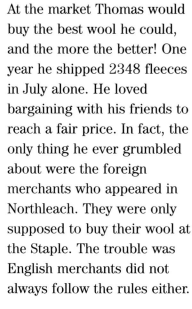

At the market Thomas would buy the best wool he could, and the more the better! One year he shipped 2348 fleeces in July alone. He loved bargaining with his friends to reach a fair price. In fact, the only thing he ever grumbled about were the foreign merchants who appeared in Northleach. They were only supposed to buy their wool at the Staple. The trouble was English merchants did not always follow the rules either.

Thomas bought wool all through the summer. In the autumn and winter he bought sheepskins as the sheep were slaughtered before the winter. After he had bought his wool, Thomas had to pack it up into bales. Bales contained about 250 fleeces. Officials appointed by the king kept a strict watch on this process. They checked the bales to make sure that no poor-quality horse hair, or even earth, had been put in to make them heavier. The royal officials sealed the bales once they were satisfied there was no cheating going on.

After that, Thomas and the other merchants transported their bales on pack horses to London, and then to ports in Essex, Kent and Sussex. Sometimes the French transported the wool to Calais. Sometimes Thomas used English ships. We know that in the month of August 1478 he hired 21 ships to transport his wool. That's a lot of wool!

4 If you could ask Thomas Betson about his work, what parts of his job do you think he enjoyed?

5 How does Source 2 support the view that the wool trade was valuable to England?

6 What information in the text supports the view that the wool trade was big business? Try to list at least three points.

7 Look at Source 4. Which of the following words describe the tone of the letter? anxious • optimistic • bored • relieved • thankful • happy

8 Look at Source 5. Is it fair to say that England was closely linked through trade to the rest of Europe? Do you find this surprising?

For Thomas, the trip across the Channel was the worst part of his job. Would his ships arrive safely? Would they sink in a storm? Would they be attacked by pirates? From Thomas's letters it seems he never suffered these fates, although we cannot be sure.

When his wool arrived in Calais, Thomas had a nervous wait while royal officials checked his bales again to make sure he had not swapped some of his fine wool for coarse wool. Once they were happy, Thomas paid his customs duties to the Mayor of the Staple, who passed the money on to the king. After that, Thomas sold it to French, Flemish, Dutch and Italian merchants. English wool was easy to sell because it was the finest wool in Europe. Flanders and England became very close partners in this period. Flemish weavers used English wool to make the finest cloth in Europe. Flemish merchants then sold the cloth all over Europe and even in Asia.

While he was in Europe, Thomas did a lot of buying as well as selling. He travelled to Antwerp and Bruges and bought goods like Flemish cloth (made from English wool), wine from Gascony, and foods like ginger and saffron. Thomas bought these things for himself and his family. However, many English merchants bought these goods in large quantities and sold them for a huge profit back in England.

Thomas's biggest headache when he was in Europe was collecting his money. It was not that his customers would not pay up. The trouble was they paid in Dutch guilders, French francs and Italian florins. Thomas often had to use a banker to work out how much he was owed in pounds. As trade grew in medieval Europe, so did the banking profession.

Thomas was a wool merchant for most of his life, although he also traded in fish as well. In 1479 he stopped trading because of a serious illness. He recovered, but died seven years later in 1486. We know from his will that he died a wealthy man and left plenty of money to look after his wife and five children.

SOURCE 4 ▼

An extract from a letter written by Thomas Betson to Sir William Stonor.

❛ And Sir, thanked be the good Lord, I understand for certain that our wool has arrived safely in Calais. **4** I would have brought this news to you myself when I came to visit, but I knew you would be anxious to hear so I write to you to tell you. ❜

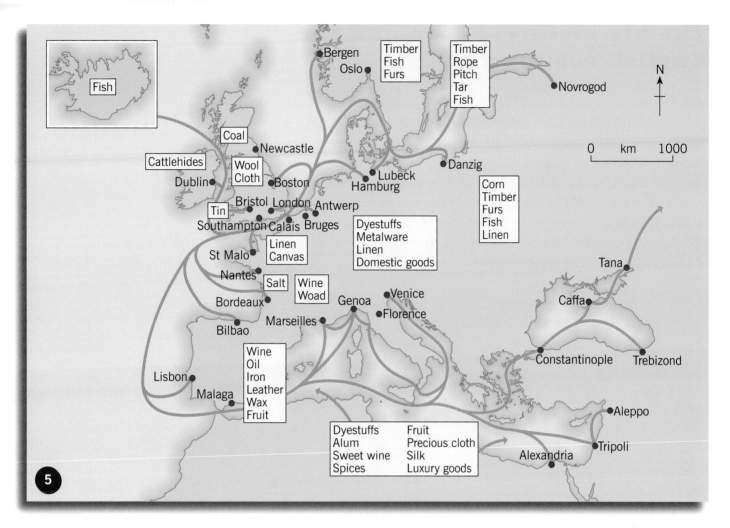

Fish

Timber
Fish
Furs

Timber
Rope
Pitch
Tar
Fish

Bergen
Oslo
Novrogod

N

0   km   1000

Coal
Newcastle

Cattlehides
Wool
Cloth
Dublin
Boston
Lubeck
Hamburg
Danzig

Corn
Timber
Furs
Fish
Linen

Bristol London Antwerp
Tin
Southampton Calais Bruges

Dyestuffs
Metalware
Linen
Domestic goods

Linen
Canvas

St Malo
Tana

Nantes
Salt
Wine
Woad
Genoa
Venice
Florence

Caffa

Bordeaux
Marseilles

Bilbao

Constantinople   Trebizond

Wine
Oil
Iron
Leather
Wax
Fruit

Lisbon
Malaga

Aleppo

Dyestuffs   Fruit
Alum   Precious cloth
Sweet wine   Silk
Spices   Luxury goods

Alexandria
Tripoli

SOURCE 5 ▲

A map of Europe in Thomas Betson's time, showing the main trade routes and the goods traded.

He also left money to his local church to repair the roof and strict instructions that his burial should be a low-key affair. The famous historian Eileen Power believed that men like Thomas were more important than many of the great knights and monarchs who dominated the history books in the 1930s when she was writing.

But let's think about the big question about why there were so many sheep at that time. If we look at Thomas Betson, the answer is that there was good money to be made in wool. But was Thomas a one-off?

Brain work

Imagine you are Thomas Betson's wife, Katherine, a few months after his death. You want your two sons, Thomas and John, to take over his business. You have to write a set of instructions explaining to them how their father worked. You may find it helpful to organise your instructions into these sections:

• Buying wool.
• Paying taxes.
• Transporting wool.
• Selling wool.

The big picture: Sheep and the English economy

Was Thomas Betson a one-off? Let's start with one of the best sources that historians have for the later medieval period – the Luttrell Psalter, which was made in the period 1320–1340. A psalter is a prayer book. The Luttrell Psalter was a book of prayers produced for an English knight from Lincolnshire called Sir Geoffrey Luttrell. It is interesting because it contains scenes of everyday life in Lincolnshire. When you look at the psalter, one thing strikes you – sheep! Even in pictures with no sheep, there are often people doing things with wool from sheep. They might be spinning, weaving, dyeing or transporting wool.

SOURCE 1a–b ▼
Scenes from the Luttrell Psalter.

1 Sources 1a–b shows the following:
   a a woman spinning wool to turn it into thread.
   b a woman milking sheep to provide milk for cheese.
   c a pen to protect sheep because they were valuable.
   d a woman carding (combing) wool to take the tangles out of it.
   Explain which activity is happening in which picture.

2 Does Source 1 suggest that sheep and wool were important to medieval people?

3 What other aspects of medieval life do these scenes tell historians about?

Overall, the Luttrell Psalter suggests that sheep played a big role in people's lives. However, one source containing a lot of pictures of sheep does not prove much. What other evidence is there that wool helped to make England rich? Look at Sources 2–5.

SOURCE 2 ▼
The house of a wealthy wool merchant who lived in Lavenham in Suffolk in the fifteenth century.

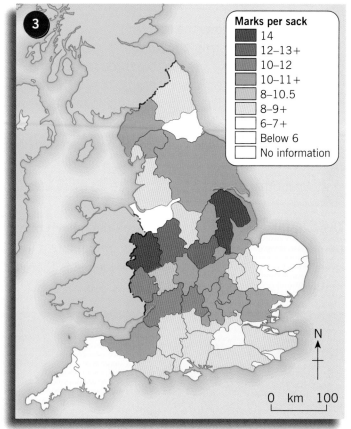

The value of wool in different areas of England in the 1340s.

By the historian Eileen Power writing in 1937.

❝ If you look at old pictures of the House of Lords in Henry VIII's reign, or Elizabeth's, you will see the woolsack in front of the throne, as you will see it in the House of Lords today. The Lord Chancellor [the top legal official in the government] is seated upon a woolsack because it was upon a woolsack that England rose to prosperity. ❞

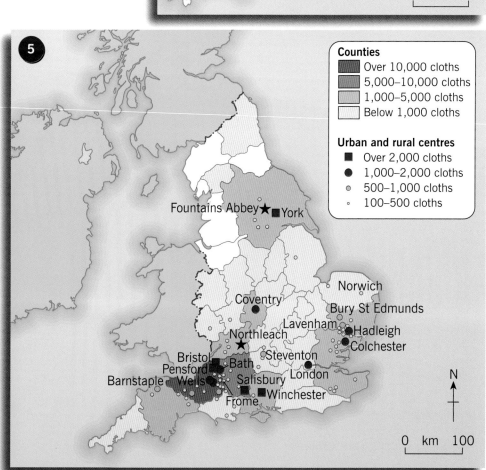

Cloth-making areas in England in around 1400. This map is based on the amount of money which the government received in tax on the cloth industry.

Brain work

So far you have looked at some sources. But that is only part of the picture. Now you have to start using the sources as evidence. Look at Sources 1–5 carefully and think about the inferences you can make from them.
The table below will help you.

Source	Key words	Inferences
	Choose from these words or come up with your own: tells, suggests, indicates, proves, denies	Choose from the list of inferences below. Warning! The statements in the list are all correct but there are too many of them so you will have to reject some!
1	This source...	
2	This source...	
3	This source...	
4	This source...	
5	This source...	

List of inferences

- That England's rulers made a lot of money from taxing the wool trade in the 1300s and 1400s.
- That English wool was the best wool in Europe and was in great demand.
- That landowners started enclosing (fencing off) land to breed sheep in the mid-1400s.
- That sheep were extremely valuable.
- That some wool merchants got very rich through the wool trade.
- That some towns gained great prosperity from the wool trade.
- That big profits were made from producing fine wool to make expensive cloth. Areas which produced the best wool got the best prices for their wool.
- That there were merchants called wool mongers who specialised in selling wool.
- That wool and cloth were part of an international trade which linked England to Europe and even further.
- That one historian believes that wool was the main factor in England's prosperity.
- That wool was important enough to be shown as a symbol of authority on important objects like official seals.

Extension work

1. As you work through the statements in the Brain work activity, look back at the text on pages 102–105. Does the information there provide evidence for any more of the inference statements?
2. 'Thomas Betson was just one successful wool trader, so his story does not prove the wool trade was important.' Do you agree with this statement? Give at least three reasons to explain your view.
3. Think back to your work on the Norman empire. Would you say England was more or less involved in Europe in Thomas's time than in Norman times?
4. Would you agree that men like Thomas Betson were just as important as kings, knights and bishops?

OVERVIEW

Henry VII is the last monarch we are going to study. In this section we are going to use him to look back at the medieval period, and the main events and developments in it.

Why does Henry VII look worried?

King Henry VII's palace, November 1508

The king woke up suddenly. A dog was barking somewhere in the palace. In truth, it did not need much to wake Henry up. He was worried. This was nothing new. Henry was a worrier, and he had always been a worrier. He worried about keeping peace and order in England. He worried in case the government was not running well. He worried about the country's finances. However, as he was getting older, what really worried him was his reputation. He wanted people to write poems and sing songs about what a great king he was.

Henry sat in the dark and thought about all the English monarchs who had gone before him. He thought about how people remembered the Norman and Angevin kings. Everyone thought of William I as the mighty conqueror. They remembered William's son Henry I as a wise ruler who improved the legal system in England. Most people knew about the great empire of Henry II and the great military skills of his son, Richard the Lionheart.

Henry thought it would be nice to be remembered like these kings. He knew they had faults. After all, Henry II had caused the murder of Archbishop Becket. But Henry VII knew that people forgot the bad side of popular kings.

SOURCE 1 ▼

A portrait of Henry VII painted in 1505.

SOURCE 2 ◄

A picture from the Luttrell Psalter showing Richard the Lionheart fighting with the Muslim leader Saladin while Richard was on the Crusades.

Henry VII smiled because he knew that people also forgot the good side of unpopular kings! Take King John. He ruled England efficiently. He collected the taxes needed to run the government. Nobody remembered these achievements. John quarrelled with the Church, and churchmen wrote the history books. As a result, people only remembered that John lost England's territories in France. They also remembered that his barons humiliated him by forcing him to sign Magna Carta.

It was a similar story with the Plantagenet monarchs. Edward I was a mighty soldier. He conquered Wales in 1283 and built a string of magnificent castles there. He almost conquered Scotland in 1305. Nobody remembered that Scotland fought back and drove the English out in 1314 at the Battle of Bannockburn. Then there was Richard II. He fought successful campaigns in Ireland. He survived the Peasants' Revolt of 1381. But people only remembered that he was cruel and harsh towards his opponents. In fact, he was so hated that he was overthrown.

Henry thought about how dangerous it was to base a king's reputation on military victories. Take the Hundred Years War between England and France. People remembered that Edward III, grandson of Edward I, was a fine soldier. He took his armies to France. He won some outstanding victories at Crécy in 1346 and Poitiers in 1356. They remembered the great victory of Henry V at Agincourt in 1415. They remembered that Henry V had almost managed to become king of France. Not many people remembered that 20 years after Henry V's death his son Henry VI lost all the French lands his father had gained.

SOURCE 3 ▲

A picture of King John from the History of England *by the monk Matthew Paris. It was produced around 20 years after John's death. John's crown is crooked because this shows that he could not rule the kingdom properly.*

SOURCE 4 ▶

A modern photograph of Caernarfon castle in North Wales. These magnificent castles reminded people of the achievements of Edward I.

'Let me describe Henry: he was taller than most men, his face fair and set on a longish neck, his body graceful, his limbs slender but marvellously strong. Indeed, he was miraculously fleet of foot, faster than any dog or arrow. Often he would run with two of his companions in pursuit of the swiftest of deer – he himself would always be the one to catch the creature. He had a great liking for music and found enjoyment in hunting, military pursuits and other pleasures that are customarily allowed to young knights. '

SOURCE 5 ◄
An extract from a book called The Life of Henry V, *written in 1437. Henry ruled from 1413–1422.*

As he thought of Henry VI, Henry VII's face took on a troubled look. He was a weak king. During Henry VI's reign, the nobles of the House of Lancaster and the House of York fought a series of vicious battles to see who would control the weak king. This was the start of the Wars of the Roses. Lancaster's symbol was a red rose, York's a white rose. The wars were fought on and off in the 1460s, 1470s and 1480s. In 1461 the Yorkist Edward IV defeated his rivals and then murdered Henry VI. He managed to survive a further challenge from the Lancastrians in 1469–1471. His rule was then stable (but not popular) until he died in 1483.

This was only 22 years before Henry VII himself had come to power. Henry remembered those events well. When Edward IV died, his young son Edward V was only 12. His uncle, Richard Duke of Gloucester was supposed to look after him. Within a few days the young king and his younger brother were dead.

Did Richard III murder the princes? He took the throne after their deaths, which made people suspicious. Richard's enemies also spread the rumour that he was a murderer. Opposition began to build up against him. Eventually a leader of the opposition emerged, Henry Tudor. Henry led an army against Richard at Bosworth Field and defeated him in 1485 (see Source 6). Henry Tudor became King Henry VII.

'The opponents of King Richard III landed at the port of Milford Haven near Pembroke in Wales, without encountering any resistance. The king was delighted – or pretended he was – when he learnt of their arrival, writing messages to all parts saying that the longed-for day had arrived when he would triumph easily over such a feeble company and that the benefits of certain peace would put new heart into his subjects.

A most savage battle now began between the two sides. Henry Tudor, earl of Richmond, advanced with his troops directly upon the king. At last, a glorious victory, together with the most valuable crown which King Richard had previously worn, was granted by heaven to the earl of Richmond, now the sole king. '

SOURCE 6 ◄
An account of the Battle of Bosworth from the History of the Kings of England. *This was written by a churchman from the Warwick area (which supported Henry Tudor). It was written during Henry's reign.*

Henry smiled at the memory. Here he was in the middle of a dark night worrying about his reputation. He knew all too well how easy it was to give a monarch a bad reputation or a good one. His friends had spent a lot of time publishing 'history books' which blackened the reputation of Richard III and gave him his bad reputation! The best way to make himself secure was to make people think that he had saved them from a terrible king (Richard III).

Henry VII hoped people would remember him as a good king. There were several things he hoped people would forget. To start with, his own claim to the throne was not very strong. He had murdered several rivals to his throne. He had not fought any glorious wars in France. On the other hand, there were things he hoped people would remember. He had stayed on good terms with the Church. England's finances were very healthy, mainly because he did not fight many wars. Most important of all, England was stable and well governed. When he died, his son Henry would not have to fight to inherit the throne. He would face other struggles.

Brain work

1 In small groups, study Sources 1–6 carefully. For each source, discuss the following questions.
  a Was the source produced at the same time as the monarch in the source was on the throne?
  b What effect would the source have on the reputation of the monarch? How does the source achieve this effect?
  c Do you think the picture sources are more or less effective than the text sources?
  d What questions would you like to ask the person who wrote or drew each source?

2 In pairs, study Sources 1–6 and the thoughts of Henry VII.
  a One of you should make a list of all the monarchs who have a good reputation and why. The other person should do the same for the monarchs with a bad reputation. You could use a table like the one below to help you.

Monarchs with a good reputation	Reasons	Monarchs with a bad reputation	Reasons

  b Come up with a list of factors which seem to affect whether or not monarchs have a good or bad reputation.
  c Look at Henry VII's record as a monarch. Explain whether you think he should look so worried!

Africa's history in two pages!

There are some important points about African history to note before you begin this unit.

- Africa is huge. The continent of Africa is bigger than the USA, China, India and Australia put together.
- African history stretches from the very first humans to recent events like the end of apartheid in South Africa.

What this means is that Africa has a lot of history and it is really important to remember this. It is important because for a long time many European and American writers said Africa did not have a proper history and that Africa's history before Europeans colonised the continent was not important.

They argued that Africans were inferior to Europeans, which helped them to justify slavery in the early 1800s. It also helped them to justify taking over the lands of African peoples in the later 1800s.

In this section you will see that Africa *does* have a history. You cannot cover it all, but you are going to select some times and places which are especially important to look at. You will look at different African civilisations and states. You will also look at how and why the history of Britain and the history of Africa are closely linked.

KEY WORDS

Continent
Empire
Inferior
Slavery

Islam in Africa
Today, most of North Africa is Muslim, and so are many other areas. You will look at how and why Islam spread so widely across Africa from the 600s onwards, and why it is still strong today.

Ancient Egypt
Egyptian civilisation (farming, towns and writing) was over 2000 years old before the city of Rome was even built. You will look at the importance of Ancient Egypt in history.

Medieval African empires
While medieval kings in Europe, like Henry II, were building empires, ruling their subjects and fighting wars, African rulers were doing pretty much the same things! You will look at how these African empires worked.

Slavery and the slave trade
Slavery was an ancient trade, but European involvement in slavery in the seventeenth and eighteenth centuries badly damaged Africa. You will look at the impact of slavery on West Africa and why the subject is still controversial today.

Scramble for Africa
In the nineteenth century many European countries took control of different areas of Africa and made them into colonies. You will look at how this affected parts of southern Africa.

Independent Africa
In the twenty-first century most African states now rule themselves. You will look at their successes and failures, and the challenges they still face in the twenty-first century.

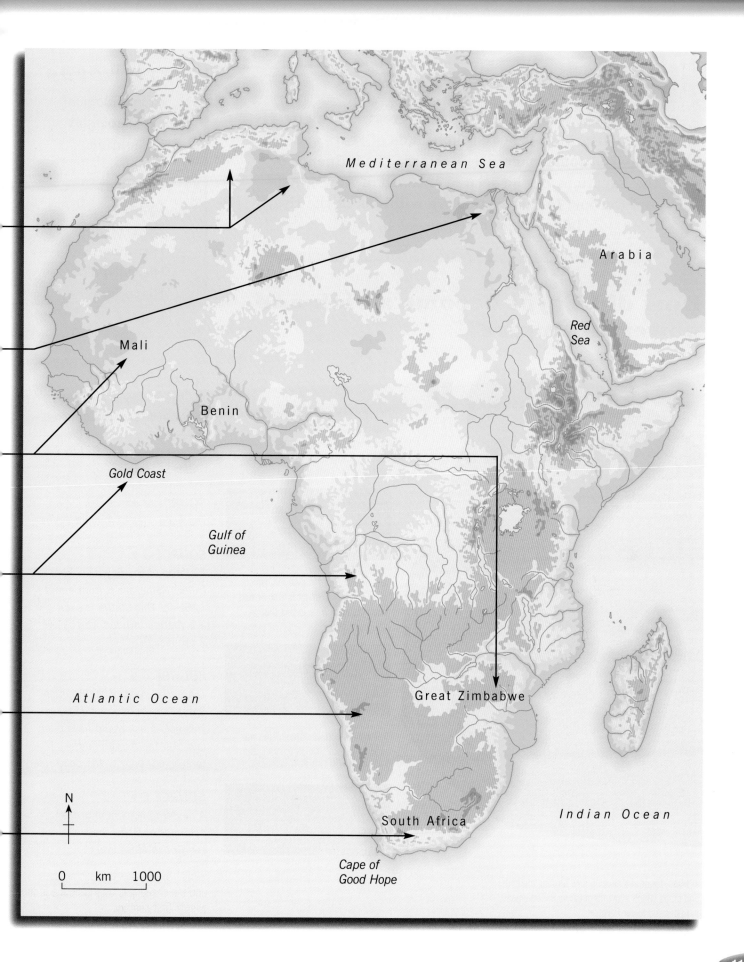

Mediterranean Sea

Arabia

Red
Sea

Mali

Benin

Gold Coast

Gulf of
Guinea

Atlantic Ocean

Great Zimbabwe

N

South Africa

Indian Ocean

Cape of
Good Hope

0   km   1000

OVERVIEW

Egypt was the first of many great African civilisations. It lasted thousands of years and achieved some magnificent things. The influence of the Egyptians can be seen over much of Africa, Asia and Europe. In this section we will look at the rise, fall and lasting legacy of Egypt.

KEY WORDS

Archaeological
Archaeologist
Civilisation
Conquer
Conquest
Dynasty
Government
Hierarchy
Hieroglyphics
Historian
Legacy

How did Egypt become a rich and powerful empire?

1

This type of script is called hieroglyphics. It used pictures rather than words. It came into use in about 3000 BC. It was the official script, used mainly by the scribes

This type of script is demotic, which came into use in about 600 BC. It was much faster to write in this than in hieroglyphics.

This type of script is Greek. This was used for administration (running the government).

SOURCE 1 ◀

The Rosetta Stone, which was carved in 196 BC. This helped archaeologists work out the different systems of Egyptian writing.

SOURCE 2 ▶

The main sites of Ancient Egypt.

SOURCE 3 ▶

A statue of the Egyptian Pharaoh (ruler) Ramesses II from about 1250 BC. This statue is over 2.5 metres tall and weighs over 7 tonnes.

SOURCE 4 ▶

The burial mask of the Pharaoh Satdjehuty from about 1500 BC. This gold mask would have been laid over the mummified (preserved) body of the dead ruler.

SOURCE 5 ▶

A modern photograph of the pyramids at Giza. These are not in the British Museum!

4000 BC: Egyptians develop new farming methods and crops which allow them to live in settlements in upper and lower Egypt.

3250 BC: Upper and lower Egypt become one kingdom under Menes.

A visit to the British Museum

You may already have studied Ancient Egypt. If you did, you may have come across some of the magnificent Egyptian objects that are in the British Museum. You may even have been lucky enough to have visited the British Museum to see the objects on display. Sources 1, 3 and 4 are just a few of them. Most of these Egyptian objects came from archaeological digs in the early twentieth century. When the archaeologists discovered them, they were amazed by how magnificent they were. They wondered how Egypt had managed to develop the wealth and power needed to make items like these. Archaeologists and historians today have a good idea how this was possible. Turn over to find out about the factors which made Egypt so rich and powerful.

Brain work

Imagine you are in the Egypt Gallery at the British Museum. You are so amazed that you phone your friend to tell them what you can see. Describe Sources 1, 3 and 4 to your friend. You should mention:

- the size and scale of the objects.
- what they are made of.
- why they were made and what they were for.

If you need more inspiration, you can see hundreds more objects on the British Museum's website at www.thebritishmuseum.ac.uk. Go to the Compass link and search using 'Egypt'.

2600 BC: Beginning of Old Kingdom – Egypt's wealth and power increases. Egyptians conquer lands to the south.

2400 BC: Pyramids built.

2100 BC: Period of instability and unrest in Egypt.

2050 BC: Beginning of the Middle Kingdom based in the city of Thebes. Middle Kingdom conquers Nubia.

Factor 1: Time

The civilisation of Ancient Egypt lasted a very long time – well over 3000 years. Egyptian historians were extremely proud of their civilisation. They measured their history in terms of the various dynasties (families) who had ruled Egypt. There were 31 of them, and over 330 rulers. Egyptian rulers were able to build on the achievements of earlier rulers. Of course, this was not always the case. Egypt had its share of problems and disasters as well as triumphs (see the timeline at the bottom of the page). However, surviving so long shows how powerful the Egyptian empire was.

KEY WORDS

Locust
Pharaoh
Ruler
Scribe
Script
Society

Factor 2: The River Nile

Ancient Egypt was built along the River Nile. Every year, the Nile flooded. As the water covered the land, it brought with it a rich, fertile mud which helped grow crops. This was the basis of Egypt's wealth. Of course, there were bad years. However, we know that as early as 2400 BC Egyptian farmers were growing about three times as much food as they needed to live on. This meant they had spare food to sell. This meant wealth, and wealth meant power!

At the top were the kings (pharaohs) and their families. They were the wealthiest and most powerful group in Egyptian society.

Below the king was an upper class. This included military leaders, priests, scribes, tax collectors, artists and scientists. This class ran the army, collected taxes, ran the government, wrote out the laws and recorded the history of Egypt. A lot of their writings survive in wall paintings, stone carvings and a few pieces of papyrus (paper made from reeds). Scribes and tax collectors travelled all over Egypt doing their job.

The farmers were at the bottom of society. They grew the food, but any surplus was taken by the upper class. This wealth was used to pay for the army. It was also used in trade, and to build the magnificent temples, tombs and other buildings.

1800 BC: Middle Kingdom attacked by nomad tribes from Asia and collapses. Nubia becomes independent.

1650 BC: Beginning of New Kingdom – Egyptian power reaches its highest point. Nubia and area to the south west are conquered.

1100 BC: Breakdown of the New Kingdom.

1050 BC: Attacks from African nomads (Berbers), who take over much of Egypt.

Factor 3: Powerful rulers

Society in Egypt was based on a hierarchy. Life for people at the bottom of the hierarchy was hard because they had to work for and obey people higher up. People at the top were powerful and stayed powerful because they could exploit those below for profit. The wealth of Egypt allowed them to keep armies. Also, Egyptian rulers persuaded their people to recognise them as gods.

SOURCE 6 ▶

A letter from an Egyptian scribe writing to a relative.

> I am told you have abandoned writing and taken to sport, and want to become a farmer. But do you not remember what happens to the farmer who is faced with paying his harvest tax when times are hard? The mice and locusts eat the crops, the cattle devour the food, the sparrows bring disaster. And then the tax collector lands on the bank. With him are guards with clubs. When they find there is no tax, the farmer is bound, beaten and ducked in the river.

Factor 4: Trade and conquest

Egyptian pharaohs were very happy trying to spread their power and influence as far as they could. The timeline below shows that Egyptian rulers conquered, lost and reconquered Nubia at different times. They also sent trading expeditions deep into Africa, probably reaching the Congo and maybe even further. At the time of the New Kingdom, the pharaoh was receiving taxes, money and gifts from many conquered lands. This in turn gave Egypt goods to trade with other civilisations in Asia.

SOURCE 7 ▼

A wall painting from the time of the New Kingdom. It shows gifts being given from Nubia to the Pharaoh Ramesses II. If you look closely you can see most of the goods which are being given.

750 BC: The Kushite people of Nubia conquer all of Egypt.

650 BC: Egypt is conquered by Assyrians, who throw out Kushites. Egyptians then regain control of Egypt.

350 BC: Greek leader, Alexander the Great, conquers Egypt.

AD 30: Romans conquer Egypt and make it a province of the Roman Empire.

1   Find a piece of evidence (a fact or a source) from pages 116–119 which shows that:

a   Ancient Egypt lasted a long time.

b   Egyptian farming was successful.

c   Life was hard for Egyptian farmers.

d   Not everyone was equal in Egyptian society.

e   Ancient Egypt was rich.

2   Look closely at Source 7.

a   Find the following items:
   • slaves • gold • animals • animal skins • ostrich eggs

b   Can you make out any other items?

Brain work

1   Imagine the British Museum needs your help! It wants to put together a leaflet to include some information and a short quiz. The leaflet will be called 'Five things that everyone should know about Ancient Egypt'.

   The trouble is, the experts at the British Museum know so much about Ancient Egypt that they cannot decide what to put in or leave out. This is where you come in.

a   In pairs or small groups, come up with a list of points about Ancient Egypt which you think everyone should know. Start by listing all the points you can find on pages 116–119. Then decide which five points are the most important.

b   You should also advise the British Museum about which pictures to include in the leaflet to make it attractive and interesting. All the pictures will need captions.

c   If you have time, you could come up with some quiz questions about Ancient Egypt. See if the rest of your class can answer them!

Extension work

By hand or using ICT, create your leaflet. Remember, it should include text, pictures and quiz questions.

2   Study the map on the opposite page and produce a summary of the main developments going on in Africa after the Roman conquest of Egypt.

How did Africa develop after the decline of Egypt?

There were many other peoples and civilisations who were in and around Africa while the pharaohs were ruling Egypt! This diagram gives a very brief outline on what was happening in Africa and the Mediterranean at the time that Egypt was declining.

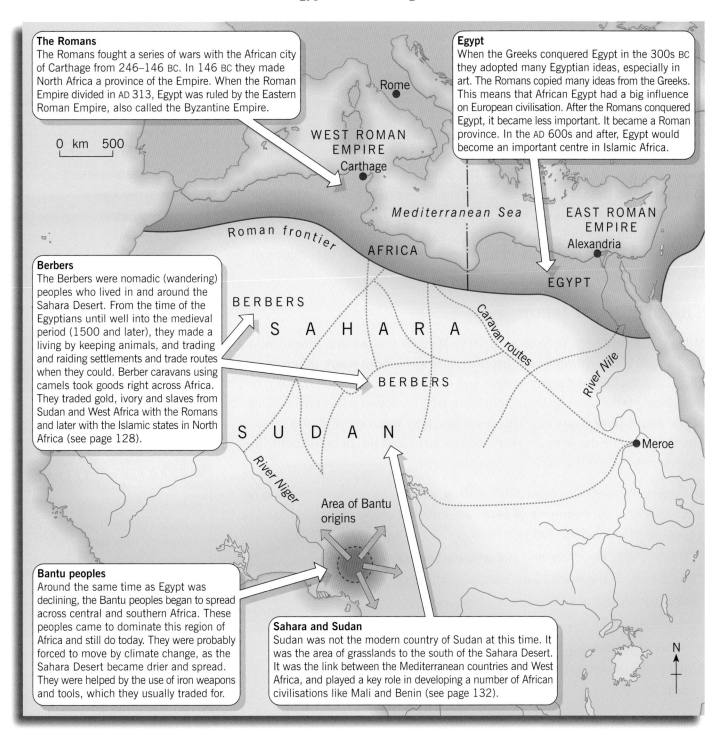

The Romans
The Romans fought a series of wars with the African city of Carthage from 246–146 BC. In 146 BC they made North Africa a province of the Empire. When the Roman Empire divided in AD 313, Egypt was ruled by the Eastern Roman Empire, also called the Byzantine Empire.

Egypt
When the Greeks conquered Egypt in the 300s BC they adopted many Egyptian ideas, especially in art. The Romans copied many ideas from the Greeks. This means that African Egypt had a big influence on European civilisation. After the Romans conquered Egypt, it became less important. It became a Roman province. In the AD 600s and after, Egypt would become an important centre in Islamic Africa.

Berbers
The Berbers were nomadic (wandering) peoples who lived in and around the Sahara Desert. From the time of the Egyptians until well into the medieval period (1500 and later), they made a living by keeping animals, and trading and raiding settlements and trade routes when they could. Berber caravans using camels took goods right across Africa. They traded gold, ivory and slaves from Sudan and West Africa with the Romans and later with the Islamic states in North Africa (see page 128).

Bantu peoples
Around the same time as Egypt was declining, the Bantu peoples began to spread across central and southern Africa. These peoples came to dominate this region of Africa and still do today. They were probably forced to move by climate change, as the Sahara Desert became drier and spread. They were helped by the use of iron weapons and tools, which they usually traded for.

Sahara and Sudan
Sudan was not the modern country of Sudan at this time. It was the area of grasslands to the south of the Sahara Desert. It was the link between the Mediterranean countries and West Africa, and played a key role in developing a number of African civilisations like Mali and Benin (see page 132).

Rome
WEST ROMAN EMPIRE
Carthage
Mediterranean Sea
Roman frontier
AFRICA
EAST ROMAN EMPIRE
Alexandria
EGYPT
BERBERS
SAHARA
Caravan routes
BERBERS
River Nile
SUDAN
Meroe
River Niger
Area of Bantu origins

0 km 500

N

OVERVIEW

Islam is the widest followed and fastest-spreading religion in Africa today. It has been important in African history since the earliest years of the religion. In this section you will look at why Islam has had such a lasting effect on so many areas of Africa.

Why did Islam spread so far and so fast in Africa?

In 622, the Prophet Muhammad left his home city of Makkah to join his companions in the city of Madinah. The people of Madinah welcomed Muhammad as the prophet of Islam. Islam has since spread far and wide and, many centuries later, it is by far the strongest faith in Africa (see Source 1). So, how did Islam come to be so important to so many millions of Africans? To tackle this question, we need to go back to the origins of Islam itself.

The origins of Islam

Muhammad was born in Makkah in 570. Makkah was an important trading city. It also had a shrine where people came to worship many different gods. Muhammad met many Jewish and Christian traders in Makkah. He was deeply influenced by their beliefs. In 610 he began to receive visions of the Angel Jibril (Gabriel). The angel told him about the will and mind of Allah (God). For the next 22 years, Muhammad told the people about these revelations.

Muhammad's messages from Allah were written down in the holy book of Islam, the Qur'an. Followers of Islam are called Muslims. Islam is based on a number of key beliefs and practices:

- There is only one God, and His will was revealed to the Prophet Muhammad. The word Islam means 'submission to Allah'.
- Muslims should pray five times a day.
- Muslims should give alms (money or food) to the needy.
- Muslims should fast during the month of Ramadan.
- Muslims should try to make a pilgrimage to Makkah at least once in their lifetime.

KEY WORDS

Arabia
Bible
Byzantine Empire
Caliph
Christian
Christianity
Islam
Jesus
Jew
Judaism
Muhammad
Muslim
New Testament
Old Testament
Pilgrimage
Prophet
Qur'an
Ramadan

Info point

Judaism and Christianity

- Judaism and Christianity are different in many ways.
- Christians believe that Jesus Christ was the Son of God. Jews do not.
- Judaism is based on the Old Testament of the Bible. Christianity is based on the Old and New Testaments. The New Testament sets out the actions and teachings of Jesus.

The spread of Islam

The rulers of Makkah thought Muhammad was a trouble-maker, and they sent over 1000 troops to catch up with him at Madinah. They were defeated by his companions. From this point, Islam gained more believers and began to spread. In 630 Muhammad and his followers conquered Makkah itself. Muhammad died two years later, but by that time the whole of Arabia had become Muslim. Muslims then chose four caliphs to lead them after Muhammad. Under these caliphs, Islam spread rapidly across large areas of Asia and Africa.

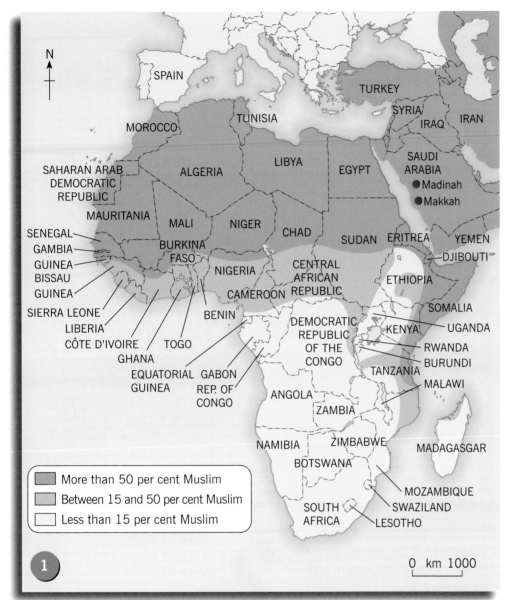

Legend:
- More than 50 per cent Muslim
- Between 15 and 50 per cent Muslim
- Less than 15 per cent Muslim

0 km 1000

SOURCE 1 ▲

A map showing the importance of Islam in Africa today.

1 Turn the information in Source 1 into words. Aim to do this in less than 25 words if you can, and do not mention the names of any countries. Some handy words might be: north • south • central • percentage

2 Describe one difference and one similarity between Christianity and Judaism.

3 What evidence is there that Muhammad's beliefs were influenced by the beliefs of Jews and Christians?

4 a From the information you have here, decide which of these words or phrases are suitable to describe Islam: peaceful • forgiving • one God • violent • good deeds • respect for Allah
   b Add some more words or phrases if you can.

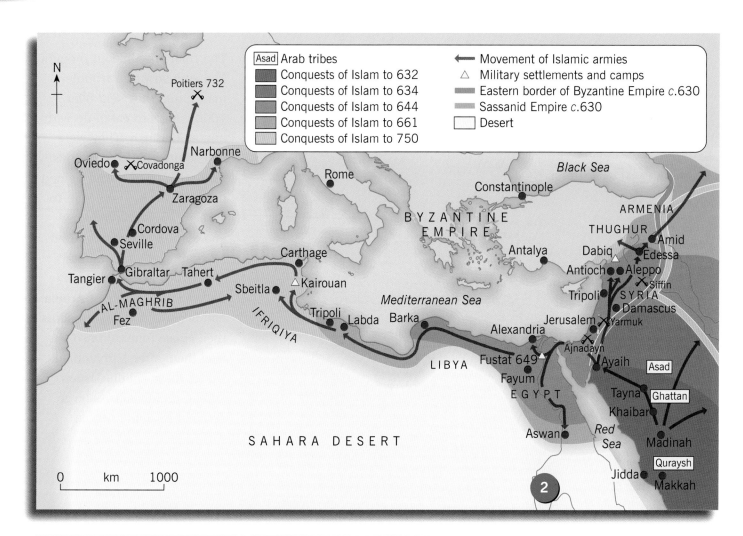

Legend:
- Asad Arab tribes
- Conquests of Islam to 632
- Conquests of Islam to 634
- Conquests of Islam to 644
- Conquests of Islam to 661
- Conquests of Islam to 750
- ← Movement of Islamic armies
- △ Military settlements and camps
- Eastern border of Byzantine Empire c.630
- Sassanid Empire c.630
- Desert

SOURCE 2 ▲
A map of Islamic conquests in Africa 632–750.

5 Look back at pages 10–23 about the spread of the Roman Empire. How does the spread of Islam compare to Rome in terms of the size of the empire and the time it took to achieve it?

How were Muslims able to achieve the amazing conquests shown in Source 2? As usual in history, there is no one, simple answer. Several factors came together.

A Muslims moved north and east and conquered lands of the Byzantine Empire in Asia. At the same time they also moved into Africa, starting with Egypt.

B Many of the Berber peoples of North Africa adopted Islam as their religion. This made the Muslim forces stronger. Many Berbers joined the Arab armies from about 710 onwards. This was one of the factors which allowed the Muslims to conquer much of Spain by 720.

C The religion of Islam united the Arab peoples and tribes. In the past, they had fought with each other. Now they followed the four caliphs.

These were Muslim leaders chosen to lead the people after Muhammad's death in 632. Once the Arabs were united, they were a very powerful force.

D The Arabs were helped because they were conquering regions where the local people hated their rulers. For example, Egypt was ruled by the Byzantine Empire. The Egyptian people were heavily taxed. They were not sorry to see the Arabs throw out the Byzantines.

E The main strength of the Muslim Arabs was their cavalry. They were able to move very fast and defeat opponents, often taking them by surprise.

F The Arabs were warlike people, skilful at fighting on horseback or on foot. Living in the desert also made them very tough.

G The Arabs developed their power at sea, and sent their forces by ship along the African coastline. This helped them to conquer the province of Ifriqiya (modern-day Tunisia) by around 700.

H Muslims were motivated by their faith. They wanted to spread Islam as far and as wide as possible. This gave them courage in battle. It also gained them allies because many Africans converted to Islam.

I The Muslim forces knew how to use weapons like ballistae. These were giant sling shots used to break down the walls of cities. The Arabs used these when they captured the Egyptian city of Alexandria in 642.

J The Arabs had a long tradition of raiding other lands. As well as spreading their faith, Muslim wars were a chance for some Arab warriors to get rich through war.

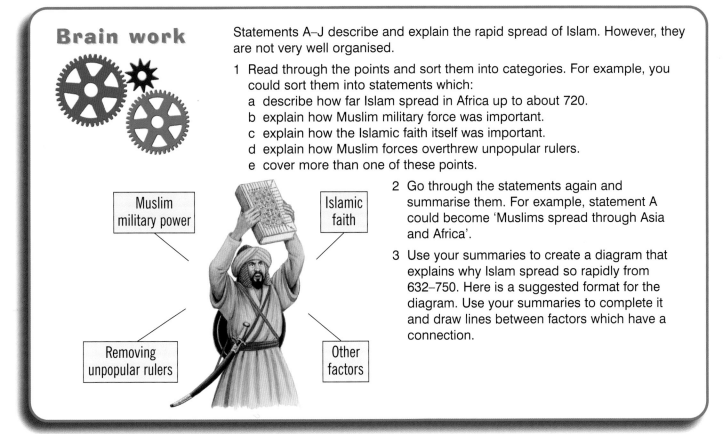

Brain work

Statements A–J describe and explain the rapid spread of Islam. However, they are not very well organised.

1 Read through the points and sort them into categories. For example, you could sort them into statements which:
   a describe how far Islam spread in Africa up to about 720.
   b explain how Muslim military force was important.
   c explain how the Islamic faith itself was important.
   d explain how Muslim forces overthrew unpopular rulers.
   e cover more than one of these points.

Muslim military power

Islamic faith

Removing unpopular rulers

Other factors

2 Go through the statements again and summarise them. For example, statement A could become 'Muslims spread through Asia and Africa'.

3 Use your summaries to create a diagram that explains why Islam spread so rapidly from 632–750. Here is a suggested format for the diagram. Use your summaries to complete it and draw lines between factors which have a connection.

Why has Islam had such a lasting influence in Africa?

Look at Source 1. You can see that the influence of Islam continued to grow after the rapid conquests of the 600s and 700s. Think back to your work on the end of the Roman Empire in Unit 1. You may remember that different parts of North Africa were ruled by the Romans, the Goths, the Vandals and the Byzantine Empire. None of these rulers had the same kind of lasting influence as the Muslims. Why was this?

SOURCE 1 ▼
The spread of Islam in Africa.

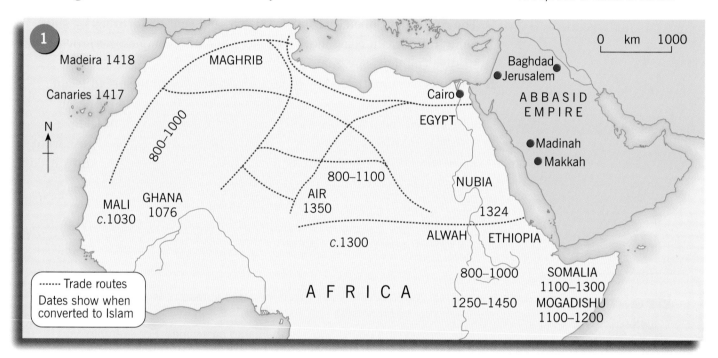

Military power

One factor was the impressive military power of the many Muslim leaders who ruled the different parts of North Africa. In Unit 2 you read about powerful kings in England and Europe like William the Conqueror and Henry II. The Muslim leaders in Africa were every bit as powerful. They had large armies and navies. They had the latest weapons and armour. King John of England once sent ambassadors to ask the Muslim leader Mohammed al Nasir for help against pirates who were attacking English trading ships.

However, Muslim military power went into decline after about 1600. From that time the Christian Europeans overtook the Muslims in terms of military strength. Islamic rule lasted much longer than Muslim military power. So this cannot be the only reason for the lasting Muslim influence.

KEY WORDS

Ambassador
Goths
Military
Mosque
Shi'ah
Sunni
Tolerant
Vandals

Beseiging a castle in 1402. This
picture was painted about 90
years after the events shown. The
drawbridge has been raised, but
the Muslim troops have made
another bridge on the right.

1 Write down one example from these pages which shows that
Muslims were powerful.

2 Discuss the following question in pairs or small groups. 'Does the
military power of Muslims explain why Islam has had such a
long-lasting influence in Africa?'

Islamic way of life

After the early conquests there were many
divisions among Muslims. Islam itself split into
two main branches, the Sunni and Shi'ah
Muslims. There were conflicts between different
Muslim leaders over who would control the
different African Muslim states.

Despite all the conflicts, there were very few
uprisings of Muslim peoples against their own
rulers. Islamic societies were divided, just like
the Christian societies in Europe. There were
rich and powerful people at the top of society.
There were poorer people at the bottom.
However, Islam was a powerful force that united
the rich and powerful Muslim rulers and the
ordinary people they ruled. This was partly
because Islam set out a code for living. All
Muslims – rich or poor – were committed to
living by this code.

SOURCE 3 ▶

An extract from Africa in History by
Basil Davidson. This is a university
textbook published in 1992.

❝In Africa, Spain and Asia Muslim conquests laid the groundwork that
could and did unite men of learning, religion and philosophy from the
Mediterranean to Arabia. What Muslim leaders could promise the people
they conquered was to belong to a new and broad community, the
ummah [community] of Islam, in which all men were of equal worth. ❞

Islam also had its own legal system. Historians have researched this in some detail. Islamic lawyers dealt with a huge range of issues ranging from divorce to disputes about who owned water wells. All the evidence suggests that the lawyers took great care to listen to all sides in these cases and make reasonable judgements. Most Islamic countries today still use Islamic law. Islam was seen as a fair way of life and so was attractive to non-Muslims.

There were also practical reasons for people to adopt Islam. On the whole, Muslims were generally more tolerant towards non-Muslims than Christians were to non-Christians. However, under Muslim rule Muslims did not pay taxes but non-Muslims did. Non-Muslims also had to accept certain restrictions (see Source 4). It made sense to become a Muslim.

3	How did Islam unite people in the Muslim states?
4	Did Islamic law work?
5	Do you think the Islamic way of life is more important than military power in explaining why Islam has had such a long-lasting influence in Africa?

Trade and prosperity

Muslims were great travellers and traders. Source 1 on page 126 shows the trade routes of the Berber peoples across the Sahara Desert. Muslim traders were a key element in linking Europe, Asia and Africa in trade. They carried basics like food and cloth; metal goods like armour, weapons and pots; and salt and gold – extremely valuable items. They traded in ivory, jewellery and different types of wood which grew in the central African forests. These cargoes were all transported by the main vehicle of the Berber traders – the camel. This amazing animal was strong, fast and could travel for long periods without food or water. There was also human cargo. North African traders carried African slaves north. There was also a trade in European slaves to Africa, mainly on Arab ships. After about 1600, North African traders began to suffer from competition from European traders who sailed direct to Africa around the African coast, missing out North Africa.

As they travelled to the black African kingdoms across the Sahara and into West Africa, the African traders took their faith with them. Great African empires like Ghana, Mali and Songhay adopted Islam (you will study Mali on pages 132–136), partly because they were impressed by Muslim beliefs. It was also because they were impressed by the wealth and stability of Muslim states. In 1324 the ruler of Mali went on a pilgrimage to Makkah. He obviously mixed trade with his pilgrimage as he took around 8000 servants, merchants and soldiers with him. He returned with 15,000 camels carrying goods like perfume, salt and jewellery. Today, much of central Africa is still Muslim.

SOURCE 4 ▼

Extracts from the Pact of Umar. *This document was first produced in the 600s. Non-Muslims signed this document and agreed to follow the rules in it.*

❛
- We shall not manifest our religion publicly nor convert anyone to it. We shall not prevent any of our kin from entering Islam if they wish it.
- We shall show respect toward the Muslims, and we shall rise from our seats when they wish to sit.
- We shall not mount on saddles, nor shall we gird swords nor bear any kind of arms nor carry them on our persons.
- We shall not sell alcohol.
- We shall not display our crosses or our books in the roads or markets of the Muslims. We shall use only clappers in our churches very softly.
- We shall not bury our dead near the Muslims. ❜

4

An extract from the Travels of Ibn Battuta, *a Muslim traveller and writer who travelled across the Muslim world in the 1350s. Here he describes travelling across the Sahara Desert.*

> At Sijilmasa [at the edge of the desert] I bought camels and a four months' supply of forage for them. I set out on February 13, 1352 with a caravan including, amongst others, a number of the merchants of Sijilmasa.
>
> After 25 days [from Sijilmasa] we reached Taghaza. Here there is a salt mine. The negroes come up from their country and take away the salt from here. The negroes use salt just as gold and silver is used elsewhere; they cut it up into pieces and buy and sell with it. The business done at Taghaza amounts to an enormous figure in terms of hundredweights of gold-dust.

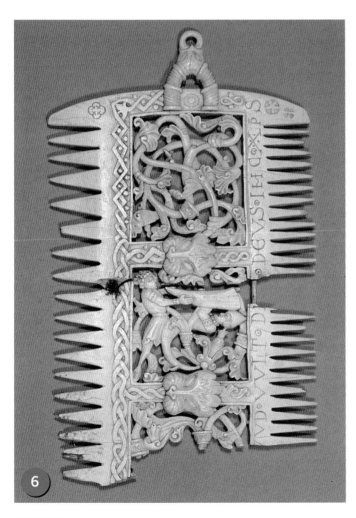

SOURCE 6 ▲

A comb carved in England in about 1100 and made from African ivory.

SOURCE 7 ▲

A brass jug made in England in the late 1300s which was used in Ghana, central Africa.

6 What goods did Muslim traders carry?

7 'Medieval England traded with medieval central Africa.' What evidence is there on these pages to support this statement?

8 How did trade help to spread Islam?

9 Does the success of Muslims as traders explain why Islam has had such a long-lasting influence in Africa?

Islamic civilisation in Africa

Muslims in Africa were not just wealthy. They also had a great civilisation with tremendous achievements. Muslim Africa was generally richer, more powerful and more developed than Europe in the medieval period. Many Muslim achievements can still be seen today.

Cities and architecture

Muslim towns and architecture are a good example (see Sources 8 and 9). The Islamic cities of Africa were full of wonderful buildings like this. Many of the buildings survive today, just like the medieval cathedrals in Europe still exist.

SOURCE 8 ◀
The Great Mosque of Kairouan, in present-day Tunisia. It was built around the same time as the Norman Conquest of England.

SOURCE 9 ▼
Koutoubia Mosque in Marrakesh, Morocco.

Education, literature and literacy

Another lasting achievement of Islam was the spread of literacy. Islam is based on the teachings in the Qur'an. For many Muslims, this was an incentive to learn to read and write the Arabic words for themselves. As more people learned to read and write, they read the Qur'an and Islam spread further. There were many other Muslim writings, of course, especially textbooks. Muslims set up many great universities in their cities and a number of these still survive today.

Science and technology

Islam made great advances in science and technology. Most Islamic cities had good water supplies, for example. Farming in the Muslim lands made extensive use of advanced irrigation techniques. You have already seen that Arabs were great travellers and traders. One of the key reasons for this was that they were great astronomers. They studied and mapped the stars very accurately. This allowed them to navigate. They also made accurate maps. European travellers and traders in the 1500s used and developed Muslim ideas to help them discover new lands, including America.

SOURCE 10 ▼
Muslim astronomers at work in a European book from the 1330s.

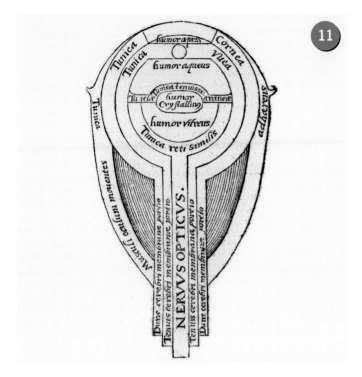

Medicine

Muslims managed great achievements in medicine and health. The Muslim faith demands that Muslims look after the sick, so most African Muslim cities had great hospitals. The Al Mansur Hospital was founded in Cairo in 1283. It had separate departments for patients with different diseases. It also had special kitchens which provided different diets for the patients, depending on their illnesses. Muslim doctors studied plants and made drugs from them. They wrote textbooks about many different diseases, and this helped good medical ideas to spread. In the medieval period, Muslims were more advanced than Europeans in this area. However, during the Crusades Europeans learnt much about Muslim medicine. From the 1200s onwards they took many Muslim ideas and developed new ideas from them.

SOURCE 11 ▲

Diagram from a Muslim medical textbook on how the human eye worked.

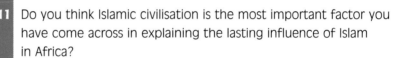

10 What did European civilisations learn from Islamic civilisation in the medieval period?

11 Do you think Islamic civilisation is the most important factor you have come across in explaining the lasting influence of Islam in Africa?

Brain work

Imagine the British Museum needs your help again! This time the department which studies Islam is putting on an exhibition. The experts cannot decide how much space to give to different aspects of Islam. They have a room which is 30 metres long and 20 metres wide. They need as much advice from you as possible on the following points:

● How much space should be given to particular areas, for example the origins of Islam, the spread of Islam in the 600s and 700s, military power, Islamic medicine?

● What images and sources could be included in the exhibition?

● What captions should go with the sources and images?

In pairs or small groups, come up with some advice for the experts. You could:

1 Write a report, *or*

2 Give a short presentation, *or*

3 Draw a plan showing how to set out the room. Include things like partitions if you think they will help visitors to get the most out of the exhibition.

OVERVIEW

In Unit 2 you studied the rise of medieval empires – powerful monarchies supported by knights, castles and similar themes. In many ways, medieval Africa was very similar. In this section you will look at two medieval African empires and the ways in which they were similar to or different from medieval times in Britain.

KEY WORDS
Colonial
Governor
Griot

How did Mali become an empire?

Source 1 gives an impression of what medieval Europeans thought of the empire of Mali. Clearly, the African ruler at the centre of the image is a powerful figure. How did Mali achieve this level of power and influence in medieval times?

Mali was not the first empire in West Africa. Between about 800 and about 1200 there had been an empire called Ghana. Ghana was like most medieval

SOURCE 1 ▼

A picture from a medieval atlas made for the King of Portugal in the late 1300s. It shows caravan traders travelling to the court of the emperor of Mali. The emperor is Mansa Mūsā, who ruled from 1312–1337. The text next to him is translated on page 136.

empires. It was a collection of powerful local rulers who were controlled by one king or emperor. In the late 1100s Ghana began to decline. The local rulers who made up the empire began to fight with each other to control the land and the trade routes, especially the valuable gold trade. In about 1203 a powerful leader called Sumanguru emerged. He was leader of the Sosso people. In 1203 he captured Kumbi Saleh, the capital of the Ghana empire.

1 Look at Source 1. The official religion of Mali was Islam. How can you tell this from the source?

2 Does the picture give any clues about the wealth of Mali?

3 Look back through the sources in Unit 2 which show British rulers. Are any of the pictures similar to this source?

4 The words to the right of the emperor are about him. Have a guess at what they say. (You can check your answer later.)

Sundiata and the foundation of the Mali empire

Sumanguru's rule did not last. In 1235 he faced a challenge from Sundiata, the leader of the Maninka people. There was a major battle at a place called Kirina. Sundiata won, and became a legend in the process (see the Info point). This life story and other evidence suggests he was an aggressive and powerful ruler.

- He conquered and took control of most of the lands which had been in the old empire of Ghana. His armies also pushed west and south and conquered new lands.
- Sundiata appointed men loyal to him to be governors in the different parts of his empire. This was similar to William the Conqueror's marcher lords (see page 62).
- Sundiata gave Mali a new constitution. This constitution set out the rights and duties of different groups in society. At the top were his military leaders – similar to knights in medieval Britain. Below them were the officials, craftsmen, free farmers and peasant farmers, and, at the bottom, were the slaves.
- Sundiata controlled the valuable trade routes. This meant that he could tax the trade in gold, ivory, iron, copper, salt and kola nuts.

Info point

Sundiata and the griots

- *Griots were the singers, poets and historians of West African society.*
- *They did not use writing, but they memorised stories as well as creating new ones.*
- *The griots of Mali created the epic* Life of Sundiata*. This story described how great Sundiata had been. It also told of how terrible Sumanguru had been.*
- *Since Sundiata ruled over the griots, we need to be careful about their stories. However, archaeological evidence suggests Mali was powerful under Sundiata.*

5 Arrange Sundiata's achievements in what you think are their order of importance.

6 In what ways was medieval Mali similar to medieval Britain?

The rise and fall of Mali

As Source 2 shows, Mali continued to develop and take control of neighbouring lands after Sundiata's death in 1260. The emperor Mansa Sakuru ruled from 1298 to 1308 and extended Mali's control over its neighbouring lands. The greatest of the Mali emperors was Mansa Mūsā. He extended the empire to its height during his reign from 1312–1337. You can find out more about him on pages 135 and 136.

Mali continued to be strong for some time after Mūsā's rule. However, by about 1400 it was going into decline. The problem for rulers who came after Mūsā was that it grew too big. It proved difficult to run effectively. It began to break up after attacks by new African empires like Songhay, and also after attacks from the Tuareg peoples of the Sahara.

SOURCE 2 ▼
The empire of Mali.

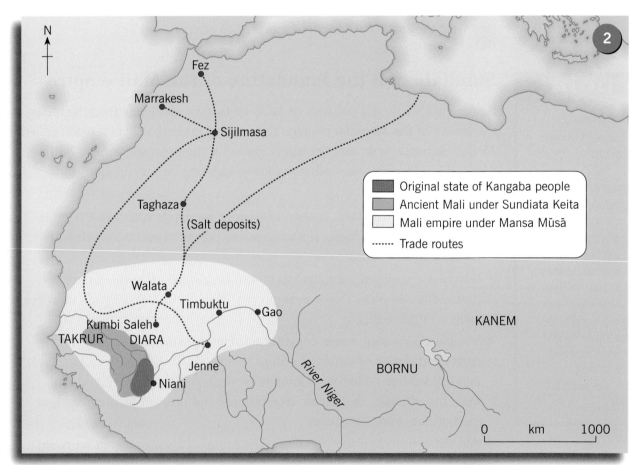

N

Fez
Marrakesh
Sijilmasa

Taghaza
(Salt deposits)

Walata
Timbuktu
Kumbi Saleh   Gao
TAKRUR   DIARA
Jenne
Niani   River Niger

KANEM

BORNU

	Original state of Kangaba people
	Ancient Mali under Sundiata Keita
	Mali empire under Mansa Mūsā
......	Trade routes

0   km   1000

---

7 Look at Source 1 on page 132 and Source 2 above. Does Source 2 suggest that Mansa Mūsā was as powerful as Source 1 seems to suggest?

8 Look again at Source 1. The words to the right of the emperor are about him. Have another guess at what they say. (You can check your answer later.)

Why was Mali under Mansā Mūsā so impressive?

Historians often have to put together a picture based on just a few scraps of evidence. The good news is that historians studying Mansā Mūsā are more fortunate. There is quite a lot of evidence on him. Much of it comes from Mūsā's own time, though some sources were made much later. The bad news is that the evidence still comes in odd scraps!

SOURCE 3 ▶
The Moroccan traveller, Leo Africanus, writing about the Mali capital of Niani in the early 1500s.

SOURCE 4 ▶
The North African writer, al-Omari, writing in around 1330.

SOURCE 5 ▶
An artist's reconstruction of a Mali trading city in the medieval period.

SOURCE 6 ▼
By Ibn Battuta, an Arab traveller in Mali in around 1370.

6 Niani is an impressive place of six thousand dwellings, and its people are the most civilised, intelligent and respected of all the peoples of the western Sudan. 9   3

6 Mūsā was the most powerful, the richest, the most fortunate, the most feared by his enemies and the most able to do good around him. 9   4

5

6 I find complete and general safety in the land, with no danger of robbery or raid. 9   6

SOURCE 7 ▶
An extract from West Africa Before the Colonial Era *by historian Basil Davidson, published in 1998.*

SOURCE 8 ▶
The North African writer, al-Omari, writing in around 1330.

6 Like the Mali rulers before him, Mūsā was a Muslim. But most of his people were not Muslims, so he supported the religion of his people as well as Islam. Different religious customs and ceremonies were allowed at his court. 9   7

6 Whenever an official has been sent to carry out an important task, the emperor questions him on everything that he did from the time he left to the time he got back, in great detail. Legal cases and appeals also go to the emperor who examines them himself. Generally, he writes nothing himself but gives his orders by word of mouth. He has secretaries and officials to write down and carry out his orders. 9   8

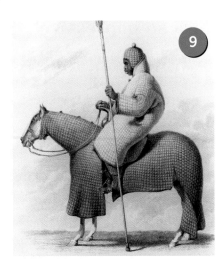

SOURCE 9 ◀

A picture of a soldier of the region which dates from 1820. Historians think this type of equipment was used by Mūsā's army. His cavalry also used bows and long swords. Arab writers claim that Mūsā had about 3000 cavalry and up to 100,000 foot soldiers.

SOURCE 10 ▶

An extract from West Africa Before the Colonial Era *by historian Basil Davidson, published in 1998.*

❝ When Mansa Mūsā came to power Mali already had firm control of the trade routes to the southern lands of gold and the northern lands of salt. Now Mūsā brought the lands of the middle Niger under Mali's rule. He brought the cities of Gao and Timbuktu within his empire. He imposed his rule on desert trading towns such as Walata. ❞

Using Sources 3–10 on pages 135 and 136, find information which will help you complete the diagram below. One section has been done to help you.

Brain work

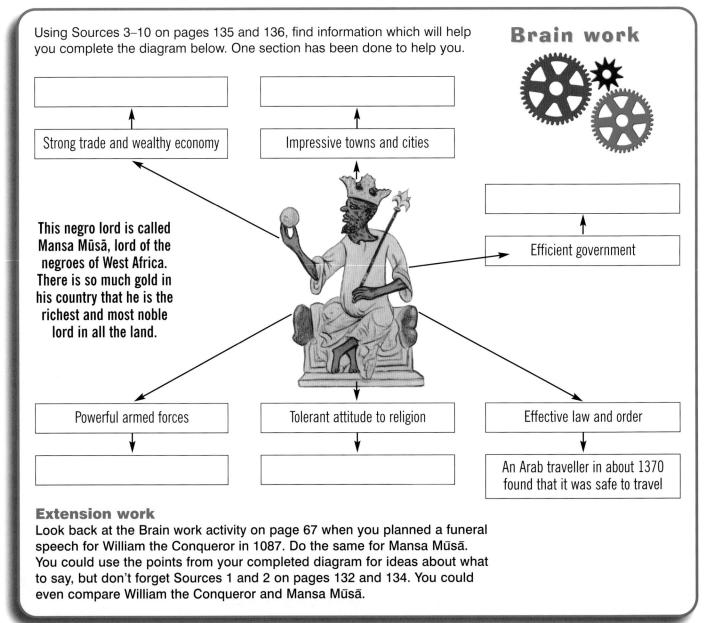

Strong trade and wealthy economy

Impressive towns and cities

This negro lord is called Mansa Mūsā, lord of the negroes of West Africa. There is so much gold in his country that he is the richest and most noble lord in all the land.

Efficient government

Powerful armed forces

Tolerant attitude to religion

Effective law and order

An Arab traveller in about 1370 found that it was safe to travel

Extension work

Look back at the Brain work activity on page 67 when you planned a funeral speech for William the Conqueror in 1087. Do the same for Mansa Mūsā. You could use the points from your completed diagram for ideas about what to say, but don't forget Sources 1 and 2 on pages 132 and 134. You could even compare William the Conqueror and Mansa Mūsā.

Why is Great Zimbabwe such a puzzle?

KEY WORDS

Fortress

Mason

Mortar

Portuguese

Settler

The first Europeans to make a big impact on Africa south of the Sahara were the Portuguese. From about 1415 they began to explore, trade and raid around the coasts of Africa. Over the next 100 years they also began to move inland. Some of the things they found amazed them. In 1531 one Portuguese explorer wrote about an astounding building he had come across in the middle of the plains of southern Africa (see Source 1).

SOURCE 1 ▶

By Viçente Pegado, captain of the Portuguese garrison of Sofala, 1531.

> **Among the gold mines of the inland plains between the Limpopo and Zambezi rivers there is a fortress built of stones of marvellous size, and there appears to be no mortar joining them. This building is almost surrounded by hills, upon which are others resembling it in the fashioning of stone and the absence of mortar, and one of them is a tower more than 12 fathoms [22 metres] high.** 1

SOURCE 2 ▶

The location of Great Zimbabwe today. It is in the country of Zimbabwe, which was named after this site. Zimbabwe means 'enclosure'.

SOURCE 3 ▶

A modern photograph of the ruins of Great Zimbabwe. The walls were about 10 metres high and 4.5 metres thick at the base.

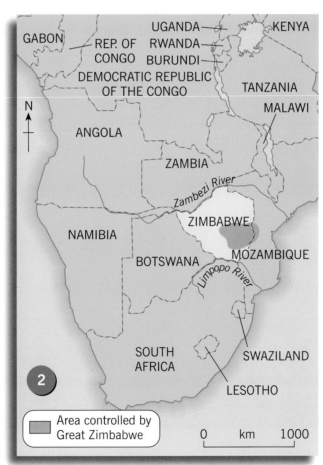

SOURCE 4 ▶

The comments of a white South African historian, M Marshall, in 1934. At this time South Africa was a segregated country in which black Africans had few rights compared with white South Africans.

> **There are no natives today living in South Africa who could have built such monumental structures. The blacks possess nothing but little huts made of wood and branches.** 4

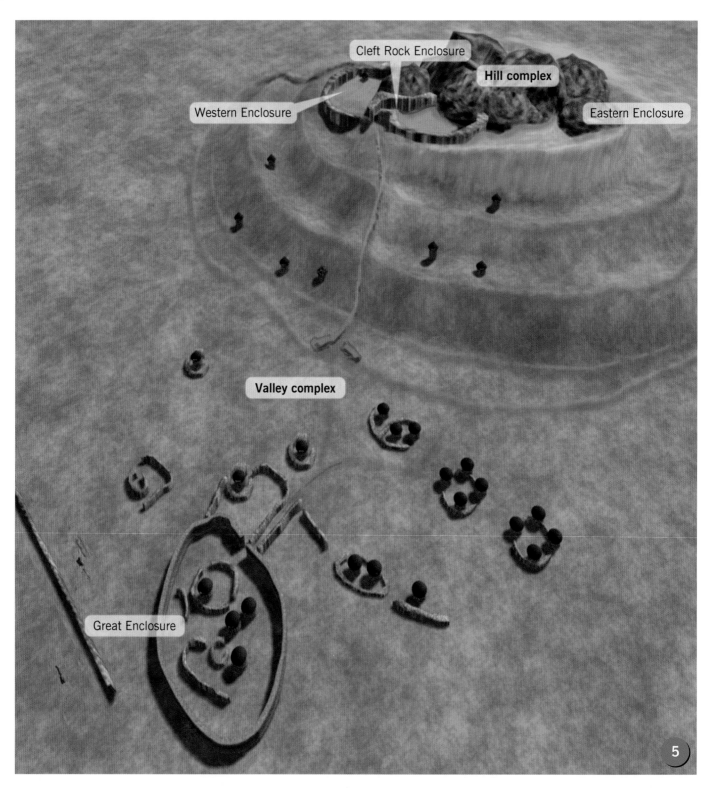

Cleft Rock Enclosure

Hill complex

Western Enclosure

Eastern Enclosure

Valley complex

Great Enclosure

5

Viçente Pegado (see Source 1 on page 137) was amazed and impressed by the size of the buildings. He was also surprised by the skill which had built them. The walls used no mortar. Masons had fitted them together, cutting the stone to the right shape. Pegado was also baffled by the location of this giant complex of buildings. It did not seem to be close to anywhere important.

SOURCE 5 ▲

An artist's reconstruction of the Great Zimbabwe site, based on archaeological evidence.

The questions

Viçente Pegado was the first of a long line of Europeans to be puzzled and fascinated by the ruins of Great Zimbabwe. The questions which kept coming up were:

- Who built Great Zimbabwe?
- When was it built?
- What was it for?
- Where did the wealth come from to build and maintain it?
- Why was it abandoned and when did this happen?

The theories

Who built Great Zimbabwe?

Viçente Pegado never got to the bottom of the mystery. Over 300 years later European explorers and settlers were still puzzling over the ruins. They came up with a range of wild theories – here are a few of them. Great Zimbabwe was built:

- by the Romans (over 6000 km away).
- by the Egyptians (over 5000 km away).
- by Solomon, the king of the Jews (over 5000 km away).
- by the Christian kings of Ethiopia (over 2000 km away).

In the early 1900s British and other European archaeologists showed clearly that Great Zimbabwe was an African settlement built by Africans. Later archaeological work showed that it was a settlement of the Shona peoples. The archaeologists also managed to work out that it was abandoned in the late 1400s. Most people agree that it was probably abandoned because the people of Great Zimbabwe exhausted their environment. Overgrazing of cattle caused soil erosion. Changes in trading patterns may also have affected Great Zimbabwe.

Despite these findings, there were still many unanswered questions about why it was built and how it supported itself. There are different theories today. Turn to the next page to read some of the theories.

---

1   Look at Sources 1–5 on pages 137 and 138. Do Sources 2–5 suggest that Source 1 was a reliable account of Great Zimbabwe in 1531?

2   a Why do you think Europeans came up with some wild theories about Great Zimbabwe?
    b How does Source 4 help to answer this question?

3   What did archaeologists find in the 1900s?

4   What have archaeologists found since the early 1900s?

139

What was Great Zimbabwe for?

Several ideas about what Great Zimbabwe was for have been put forward.

- **Theory 1**: It was a religious site. Local Africans brought offerings of ivory and gold to the site. This attracted Arab traders from ports in East Africa. Trade made Great Zimbabwe rich and this explains why such a magnificent site developed.

- **Theory 2**: It was a trading centre. The area around it was rich in copper and other minerals. Local chiefs became wealthy through trade. They used their wealth to build Great Zimbabwe to show off their power and status – and to have a nice place to live!

- **Theory 3**: It was a trading and farming centre. It was built by local rulers who controlled farming and trade in the region around it. Their main advantage was that the local area was free of the tsetse fly which caused sleeping sickness. As farming prospered, they were able to trade. As trade and farming prospered, the rulers of Great Zimbabwe became rich. This allowed them to build an impressive place to live.

Historians and archaeologists are still divided about these theories. They have found lots of facts and figures but many of these seem to support more than one theory. See for yourself.

Facts and figures about Great Zimbabwe

A Great Zimbabwe is the largest of a collection of about 150 settlements. It looks like Great Zimbabwe was the capital of this region, and ruled the people in it.

B The walls of Great Zimbabwe and the other settlements were built without mortar. This needed great skill in working stone, possibly specialist craftsmen.

C The stone buildings went up in around 1250–1300. The settlement itself had been used by people from about 1000.

D Most archaeologists think that the stone buildings inside the walls were lived in by high-status people (for example, kings or priests).

E Most people probably lived in simple mud and grass cottages. Any remains of these were destroyed by weather, animals and treasure hunters looking for gold.

F In a rubbish pit archaeologists found 1330 animal skeletons. The great majority of them were cattle.

G It seems that there was competition for the best land. Archaeologists think that the top people in society got the best land and the poorer people had to work it for them. They also got the poorer land for themselves.

H Estimates suggest that around 18,000 people may have lived in and around the city.

I No sewerage facilities have been found. This suggests pollution and disease may have been a problem.

J Evidence suggests that the growth of Great Zimbabwe came at the same time as the growth of trading ports on the east coast of Africa. Great Zimbabwe's decline came at the same time as these eastern African ports began to decline (from around 1450 onwards).

K Goods found at Great Zimbabwe include glass bowls from Arabia and dishes and pottery from China. However, archaeologists found much larger collections of local goods like ivory, gold and copper.

L Archaeologists have also found many remains of sculptures and ornaments. These may have been for decoration or they may have been used in religious ceremonies.

Brain work

1 In pairs or small groups, look carefully at all the points made under Facts and figures about Great Zimbabwe. Decide which of theories 1–3 is best supported by the evidence. You could use a table like this to help you.

Points which could support theory 1	Points which could support theory 2	Points which could support theory 3

2 Which theory do you think is most likely to be right? Explain your choice. (Remember that the experts cannot decide which theory is right, so don't worry if you cannot decide! Just make sure you can say why you cannot make up your mind.)

SOURCE 6 ▶

By a British historian writing in 1966 in a book called The Rise of Christian Europe.

❝ **Perhaps in the future there will be some African history to teach. But at present there is none or very little. There is only the history of the Europeans in Africa [from about 1600].** ❞

6

Brain work

Read Source 6. When the historian made these comments in 1966, they caused outrage among Africans and historians of Africa. Look back at your work on pages 137–141 and write a response to this view. You could set it out along these lines.

> *I am not convinced by Source 6. My studies have shown me that there is plenty of African history to study and plenty of source material available to study that history.*
>
> *Examples of African history which could be studied include...*
>
> *There is also plenty of source material. For example...*

OVERVIEW

In this section you will look briefly at the slave trade in Africa's history. The focus will be on how slavery worked in Africa, and how slavery affected Africa and Africans.

KEY WORDS

Americas
Campaign
Loathsome
Resistance
Slave trade
Suffocate
Trauma

One experience of the slave trade

" One day, when all of our people were gone out to their works as usual, and only I and my dear sister were left to mind the house, two men and a woman got over our walls and in a moment seized us both; and, without giving us time to cry out, or make resistance, they stopped our mouths, tied our hands and ran off with us.

[Equiano was then sold to a series of African slave traders who took him to a sea port to sell him to European slavers. He lived on a slave ship while the captain bought a full cargo of slaves. Sometimes this took weeks.]

I was soon put down under the decks, and there I smelt such a smell as I had never experienced in my life. I now wished for the last friend, Death, to relieve me; but soon, to my grief, two of the white men offered me eatables; and, on my refusing to eat, one of them held me fast whilst the other flogged me severely. I saw other prisoners most severely cut for attempting to jump in the water, and hourly whipped for not eating.

[Once the slave ship had a full cargo of slaves it set sail.]

Now the whole ship's cargo were confined together. The closeness of the place and the heat of the climate, added to the number in the ship which was so crowded that each had scarcely room to turn himself, almost suffocated us. The air soon became unfit for breathing, from a variety of loathsome smells, and brought on a sickness among the slaves, of which many died, thus falling victims to the unwise greed, as I may call it, of their owners. "

SOURCE 1 ◀

Olaudah Equiano describes his experiences of slavery in the 1700s. He was born in about 1745 and captured by slave raiders when he was 11 years old.

SOURCE 2 ▼

A portrait of Olaudah Equiano produced in 1789.

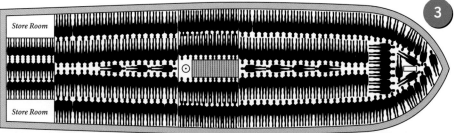

Store Room

Store Room

SOURCE 3 ◀

A diagram produced by anti-slavery campaigners in the early 1800s showing how slaves were packed on board ships.

The experience of the African who wrote Source 1 was both typical and untypical. He was typical in that he was captured in a slave raid by neighbouring African peoples and then sold into slavery. He was typical in that he suffered. He was also typical in that he resisted slavery in the most effective way he could.

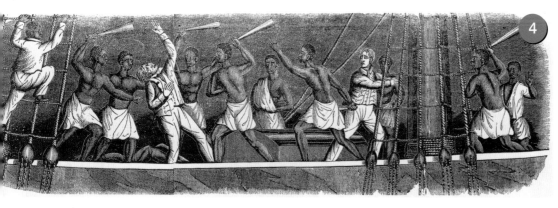

SOURCE 4 ▲

A slave revolt on board the slave ship Amistad *in 1839. Revolts on ships were common. They were one reason why slaves were treated so harshly.*

However, at this point Equiano starts being untypical. He served a ship's captain so he travelled all over the world. He also learned to read and write. His education and talents allowed him to buy his own freedom. He came to England, settled and got married. He campaigned against slavery by writing and making speeches.

Olaudah Equiano is an important source for historians studying slavery. But he is just one individual in a huge story. This story involves millions of Africans and covers Europe, Africa and the Americas (North and South).

1 Read Source 1.
  a How did Equiano become a slave?
  b Did slavery exist in his country?
  c In what ways did Equiano suffer on the slave ship?
  d Why did Equiano think that the slave owners were unwise and greedy?

2 Look at Source 3. In what ways does it back up or contradict Equiano's story in Source 1?

3 Look at Sources 2 and 4. What do these sources tell you about how Africans reacted towards slavery?

Brain work

Imagine you are working for a newspaper in the late 1700s which opposes slavery. Write a short article (about 75 words) to support your case. You should choose evidence and examples which will make the biggest impact in a short space.

How did slavery become such a major part of Africa's history?

Look back at Source 1 on page 142. Historians do not know how many Africans suffered the same experience as Equiano. Estimates vary from about 8 million to 15 million. What we do know is that the transatlantic slave trade was appalling. Around 10 to 20 per cent of the slaves died on the way across the Atlantic, mainly from disease. When they reached the Americas, they were treated badly. Slaves in the Americas generally had no rights. Slaves in Africa usually had some rights. They could earn their freedom. They could marry into the families of their owners. It was not unknown for them to inherit their owner's properties. The Mali emperor, Mansa Sakuru, who ruled from 1298 to 1308, was a freed slave.

So, how did the Africans allow this terrible trade to happen? To understand this, you need to look at several factors.

Slavery in Africa

Slavery had *always* been a big part of African history. You have already seen that Africans were traded as slaves with Ancient Egypt and with the Muslim kingdoms in North Africa. Slave trading continued across the Sahara to North Africa throughout the nineteenth century. There was a big trade in slaves

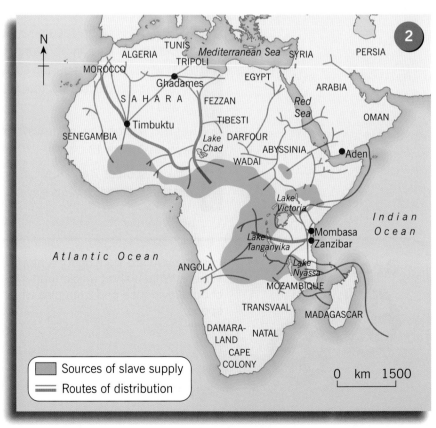

Sources of slave supply
Routes of distribution

from East Africa to Arabia. From about 1500 European traders (mostly from Portugal) also started to get involved in the slave trade. They took slaves to Europe and America. At first this trade was on a fairly small scale. However, it continued to grow over the next 300 years.

Europeans and the transatlantic trade

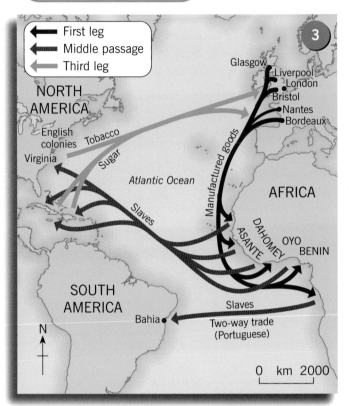

The biggest reason for the growth was on the other side of the Atlantic Ocean. From the 1500s to the 1700s Europeans explored and conquered much of North and South America. Spain and Portugal controlled large territories in South America. France and Britain controlled much of North America and the Caribbean. These lands were often called 'the Americas'.

The Europeans wanted to make money out of the Americas. They needed workers who could work in tropical conditions. They needed workers with skills in mining (mainly gold and silver), metal working and farming. Many Africans had these skills so Europeans bought them as slaves. African slaves dug the mines and farmed the tobacco plantations of South America. They also made fortunes for British and French owners of sugar plantations in the West Indies. They brought the techniques of growing rice from West Africa to areas of North America like South Carolina.

SOURCE 1 ◀

A print published by opponents of slavery in Britain in the early 1900s. The irons worn by the slave were a common punishment for trying to escape.

SOURCE 2 ◀

The slave trade in Africa around 1900. The trade continued long after slavery became illegal in the British Empire in 1833.

SOURCE 3 ▲

The transatlantic slave trade at its height in the mid to late 1780s.

SOURCE 4 ▶

The accounts of a Scottish slave trader in the 1760s.

1 How many Africans were transported across the Atlantic, and why is it so hard to be sure about the numbers?

2 Were slaves in Africa treated better than slaves in America?

3 Where were the main slave trade routes in Africa?

4 Why did the Europeans need more slaves in the 1500s and 1600s?

5 What did African slaves contribute to the development of the Americas?

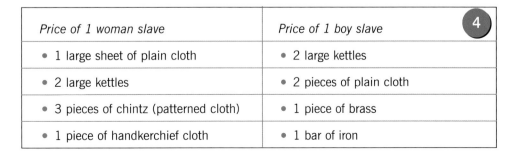

Price of 1 woman slave	Price of 1 boy slave
• 1 large sheet of plain cloth	• 2 large kettles
• 2 large kettles	• 2 pieces of plain cloth
• 3 pieces of chintz (patterned cloth)	• 1 piece of brass
• 1 piece of handkerchief cloth	• 1 bar of iron

European merchants found they could make huge profits from the trade in slaves. In Europe alcohol, glass goods, cloth, guns, tools, pots and many other items were being made cheaply in factories or workshops. The Europeans brought these goods to the coast of West Africa and traded them for slaves. French, British, Dutch and Portuguese traders competed with each other to buy slaves throughout the 1600s. By the mid 1700s the trade was dominated by Britain. As Source 7 shows, it was not always honest. Bristol, Liverpool and London grew extremely rich from this trade. The money went into new industries and created jobs in factories for workers making guns, cloth and the other goods which were sent to Africa.

SOURCE 5 ◀

A British trading fort on Africa's west coast in about 1750. These forts were to defend goods and slaves from pirates and other Europeans rather than to defend against Africans. Slaves were held in these forts until ships were ready to sail. The slaves were then ferried out in large canoes.

Few articles are delivered genuine or entire. The spirits [traded for captives on the coast] are diluted by water. False heads are put into the kegs that contain the gunpowder; so that, although the keg appears large, there is no more powder in it than in a much smaller one. The linen and cotton cloths are opened, and two or three yards, according to the length of the piece, cut off: not from the end but out of the middle, which is not so readily noticed.

The natives are cheated in the number, weight, measure or quality of what they purchase in every possible way. And thus the natives become jealous and revengeful, particularly with the English (I am sorry to add).

For so far their vindictive temper is restrained by their ideas of justice. They will not often revenge an injury received from a Liverpool ship upon one belonging to Bristol or London.

For, with a few exceptions, the English and Africans consider each other as villains who are always watching opportunities to do mischief. In short we have, I fear too deservedly, a very unfavourable character upon the Coast. When I have charged a black with unfairness and dishonesty, he has answered if able to clear himself, with an air of disdain, 'What! Do you think I am a white man?'

SOURCE 6 ▲

A typical slave ship of the type that took Equiano to America. In the bottom panel of the picture the British slave traders are buying slaves from the African slave dealers.

SOURCE 7 ◀

An extract from Thoughts Upon the Slave Trade, *written by John Newton in 1788. Newton was a slave trader who later supported the campaign to abolish slavery.*

6 What goods did the Europeans trade for slaves?

7 Read Source 7.
   a What does it tell you about the goods traded in the slave trade?
   b What does it tell you about relations between Europeans and Africans?
   c John Newton was opposed to slavery by the time he wrote this source. How does that affect your view of the source?

Africans and the slave trade

By the 1760s over 80,000 slaves per year were being captured and transported across the Atlantic. The slave traders did not capture the slaves themselves. They were supplied by African rulers like the kings of Asante and Dahomey.

SOURCE 8 ▶

An estimate of the numbers of slaves transported from Africa to America, 1701–1820.

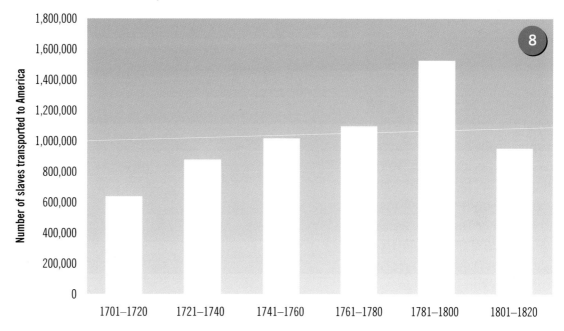

Some African rulers had concerns about the slave trade. For example, the rulers of Benin resisted the demands of slavers for more slaves in the 1650s. However, Benin's neighbours in the Oyo kingdom simply supplied the Europeans with the extra slaves they wanted. In the 1700s the rulers of Kongo and Angola also fought the slave trade. They too found that their neighbours supplied the traders with what they wanted.

9

Captured slaves being driven to the coast to be sold to European traders.

SOURCE 10 ▼
A drawing of a slave raid produced by opponents of the slave trade in 1809. It is very likely that the raiders would have been using guns rather than spears.

Many other African rulers did what the Oyo kings did – they supplied slaves to the Europeans. This was because there were huge profits in the trade. For example, in the 1750s King Tegebesu of Dahomey earned around £250,000 a year from slavery. In Dahomey the slave trade was run by the kings. All slave trading had to pass through the port of Ouidah (see Source 11). The Dahomey kings controlled this port.

10

SOURCE 11 ▶

*An extract from the journal of
John Atkins, a Royal Navy doctor
writing in 1721.*

❝ **Ouidah is the greatest trading Place on the Coast of West Africa, selling off as many Slaves, I believe, as all the rest together; 40 or 50 Sail (French, English, Portuguese, and Dutch) freighting there every year. The King sometimes makes fair Agreements with his Country Neighbours but if he cannot obtain a sufficient number of Slaves that way, he marches an Army, and depopulates [removes people]. He, and the King of Ardra adjoining, commit great Depredations [raids] inland.** ❞

11

The kingdoms of Oyo and Dahomey grew powerful by raiding their neighbours for slaves and selling them to the Europeans. The British, French and Portuguese also built up political alliances with nations like the Asante. They helped them against their enemies. This often made the wars between the African kingdoms worse, but it created new supplies of slaves. As the historian Walter Rodney put it, 'the African ruling class joined hands with the Europeans in exploiting the mass of ordinary Africans'.

Brain work

Look back at Source 3 on page 145. This map shows the items that were transported and where they went. However, it leaves out a lot of information. Your task is to redraw this map and label it so that it contains more information. Your diagram should give enough information to allow someone to answer these questions:

- Who was involved in the slave trade?
- What did they sell and who did they sell it to?
- What did they buy and who did they buy it from?
- Who gained from the slave trade?
- Who lost from the slave trade?

Some of the people you might want to mention are:

- British, Portuguese and French slave traders.
- African slave traders.
- The rulers of Oyo, Benin, Dahomey and Asante.
- Owners of mines and plantations in the Americas.
- Ordinary people in Europe's towns and cities.
- Ordinary Africans.

Extension work

Experiment with presenting the same information in different ways. For example, write a report or draw a cartoon strip about the slave trade. You could use the sources on pages 142–148 as your visual images, or you may be able to research your own images. Which way of presenting the information is the most effective?

What was the impact of the slave trade on Africa?

The slave trade had a devastating impact on Africa in the eighteenth and nineteenth centuries, but it also left a legacy that reaches far beyond Africa today.

The impact of slavery on Africa: Then

Transatlantic slavery reached its peak in the 1780s. Slave trading was abolished in the British Empire in 1807, and slavery itself was abolished in 1833. However, slave trading carried on long after that. It was not abolished in the USA until 1865, so there was still a trade in slaves across the Atlantic Ocean. The slave trade to Arabia continued well beyond that time.

Depopulation: One effect of the trade was depopulation. Africa lost something like 10–12 million inhabitants to slavery. The wars to gain those slaves probably cost many more millions of lives. Population growth in Africa was much slower than it was in Europe in the period 1700–1900.

Political chaos: As you have seen, the slave trade was fed by wars and raids. The British explorer David Livingstone believed that ten Africans died for every one slave who was sold. A key element in this process was the gun trade. It created a vicious circle (see below).

Loss of best workers: The slaves taken were generally the young men and women who were the most productive members of society. They had skills in mining, metalworking and farming. The loss of these valuable workers held back economic growth in Africa.

Under-development of African industry: In return for slaves, Africans received European manufactured goods like cotton cloth. This undermined the development of the cotton industry in Africa. This was also true of other industries like metalworking. As a result, African industries did not develop, while European industries did. Slavery made Africa dependent on European industries for goods instead of developing its own.

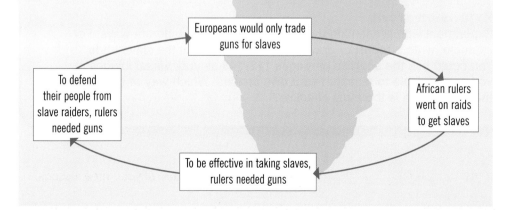

Europeans would only trade guns for slaves

African rulers went on raids to get slaves

To be effective in taking slaves, rulers needed guns

To defend their people from slave raiders, rulers needed guns

KEY WORDS

British Empire
Depopulation
Vicious circle

SOURCE 1 ▼
An extract from an article called Slave trade: a root of contemporary African crisis *by Tunde Obadina, published in 2000. Tunde Obadina heads a British charity called Africa Business Analysis, which publishes articles about African issues.*

❛ It was during the slave trade and slavery that white people began to think they were superior to blacks. It is not difficult to understand why white traders who bought black people for the price of watered-down brandy and packed them onto slave ships like cattle could consider themselves to be superior. As the centuries passed Europeans became more and more scornful of black people. During the slave trade Africans came to believe themselves to be inferior. They lost confidence in themselves, their culture and their ability to development. ❜

The kingdom of Asante had an army of about 80,000 men, about half armed with guns. Dahomey had about 12,000 men, all armed with guns. Other states were not so powerful, but they still carried out raids. The wars became so common that many African states began to disintegrate. This gave Europeans, especially Britain and France, the chance to step in, take over and 'restore order' as they saw it.

The impact of slavery on Africa: Now

Slavery is a historical topic that still has an important legacy today. Perhaps the two biggest issues connected with slavery are the economic condition of Africa today, and the problem of racial prejudice which many Africans still face, especially in Europe and America (see Sources 1 and 2).

SOURCE 2 ▶

Dr Akousa Perbi, a historian at the University of Ghana, writing in 1999 on the issue of slavery.

' **Right now the legacy of the slave trade is still with us. We must remember that slavery was abolished [in the British Empire] in 1807, but in this part of the world the whole process took about a hundred years to come into effect. So we are talking really about 1907, 1908 when it all ended. That's only 90 years ago – remember that for about 400 years slavery had been going on. We've destroyed a lot of things, socially, economically, politically. There are still some areas** ② **in the northern part of Ghana which are depopulated right now because of the transatlantic slave trade. So we are putting up with this legacy right now. And it's important to realise that. But the point is, as historians, we have to tell the story as it was [including the involvement of Africans] so that we don't repeat the mistakes of the past.** '

Brain work

Slavery is a very sensitive issue. In some countries, it is too sensitive to teach. Other countries are beginning to wonder how to teach it.

Imagine you are a history teacher and you have to teach slavery for the first time. You have three lessons for the whole topic, so you are going to have to select what you teach.

1 Work through pages 142–151 again and make rough notes of all the important points you have come across on these pages.

2 Sort out these points using a table like the one below.

Points about the slave trade which are essential	Points about the slave trade which are important and interesting but not essential	Points about the slave trade which are very sensitive, so need careful explanation	Points about the slave trade which can be left out

3 Come up with a short plan of what you will teach in each of your three lessons.

OVERVIEW

The slave trade built close trading links between European states and African rulers. In the nineteenth century, the European states went beyond these links. They took control of the whole continent of Africa. In this section you will look at how this happened. You will also look at the effects of colonialism on Africa as a whole, and on South Africa in particular.

KEY WORDS

Colonialism
Colony
Critic
Patronising

SOURCE 1 ▼

A map showing the takeover of African lands by European states by the early 1900s.

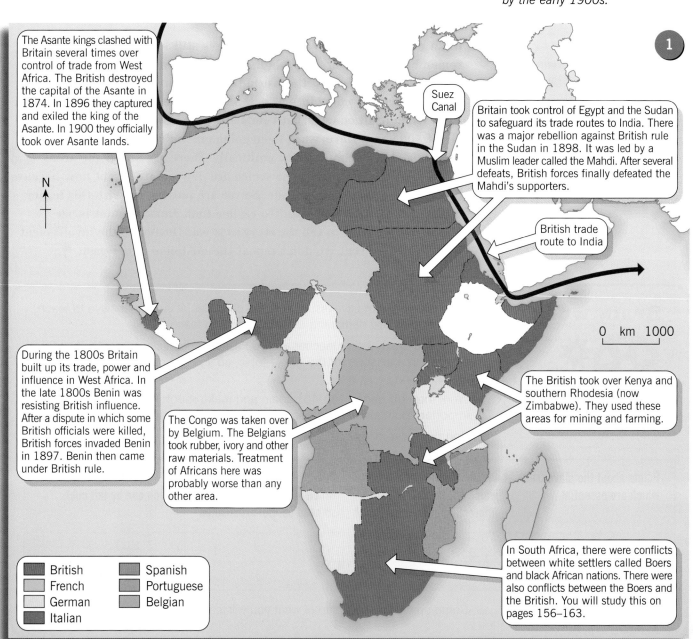

The Asante kings clashed with Britain several times over control of trade from West Africa. The British destroyed the capital of the Asante in 1874. In 1896 they captured and exiled the king of the Asante. In 1900 they officially took over Asante lands.

Suez Canal

Britain took control of Egypt and the Sudan to safeguard its trade routes to India. There was a major rebellion against British rule in the Sudan in 1898. It was led by a Muslim leader called the Mahdi. After several defeats, British forces finally defeated the Mahdi's supporters.

British trade route to India

During the 1800s Britain built up its trade, power and influence in West Africa. In the late 1800s Benin was resisting British influence. After a dispute in which some British officials were killed, British forces invaded Benin in 1897. Benin then came under British rule.

The Congo was taken over by Belgium. The Belgians took rubber, ivory and other raw materials. Treatment of Africans here was probably worse than any other area.

The British took over Kenya and southern Rhodesia (now Zimbabwe). They used these areas for mining and farming.

0   km   1000

In South Africa, there were conflicts between white settlers called Boers and black African nations. There were also conflicts between the Boers and the British. You will study this on pages 156–163.

British	Spanish
French	Portuguese
German	Belgian
Italian	

What was the Scramble for Africa and what did it mean for Africans?

In the late 1800s and early 1900s, European powers competed with each other to build empires in Africa. Africa became a collection of European colonies (lands ruled by Europeans). The race to build African empires became known as the Scramble for Africa. Source 1 shows the results of the Scramble. We are now going to concentrate on the British Empire in Africa. Let's start by looking at why Britain took over so much of Africa.

- **Wealth and power**: Britain wanted to develop trade in certain goods, control trade routes or take over valuable resources. This often caused arguments with African rulers, which led to wars. Wars led to conquest by well-armed British forces.

- **Individuals**: In some areas, British conquests were the result of the ambitions of British explorers, adventurers or soldiers. The British government did not always have complete control of its people in Africa.

- **Christianity**: In many areas the first British people to arrive were missionaries. They wanted to bring Christianity to Africans. They set up communities, often based around a mission school or hospital.

- **Civilisation and good order**: Many explorers, missionaries, officials and soldiers genuinely believed they were bringing civilisation to Africa. They were usually unaware of past African civilisations or traditions. When they did know about past African civilisations or traditions, they ignored them. They were convinced that their own values and ideas were best. They saw it as their duty to try to make Africa like Britain.

- **Settlement**: In some areas white Europeans came to build new lives, usually as farmers but sometimes in mining.

Brain work

What were the motives of the men and women who built Britain's empire in Africa? Historians have found many different motives for British involvement in Africa. They could be summed up as follows:

- They were selfish.
- They were trying to do good.
- They were trying to do good but in a patronising way.

Look at the information on these pages and see whether you can find any facts or events to support these points. Sum up your findings in a diagram like the one shown here.

Was British colonial rule a positive or negative experience for Africans?

Colonies are pieces of land and countries ruled by another country. As you saw on page 152, the British (and other Europeans) ruled over many colonies in Africa. How did Africans feel about this?

You will not be surprised to find out that opinions on this issue are divided. Most African historians generally believe that colonial rule did more for Britain than it did for Africa. Other historians would disagree. A lot depends on how you interpret the evidence. For example, look at Source 1.

> An admirer of British rule would say that it brought job opportunities and enough money to buy guns and blankets

> A critic of British rule would point out that this picture shows a patronising and insulting attitude towards the Africans

> A critic of British rule would say that the jobs the Africans were doing were poorly paid and dangerous

1 Which parts of Source 1 would the critic regard as patronising or insulting?

2 Is there any evidence in Source 1 to support the view that mine work was dangerous?

3 The original artist of Source 1 was trying to present a positive view of British rule in Africa. Explain how he has tried to do this.

SOURCE 1 ▲
A British picture from 1873 called The natives before and after working in the mines in Kimberley, South Africa. *It suggested that working in the mines turned Africans from 'savages' (on the left) into prosperous workers (on the right).*

Colonialism created new states like Nigeria, which lumped together different African nations with different languages and traditions. This is one of the reasons why some African states are still unstable today.

Africans got new job opportunities in cloth and mining.

British rule brought the development of new towns and the growth of existing towns. This created jobs for Africans.

Africans were being ruled by foreigners and this was humiliating.

The jobs most Africans got in industries were usually low paid and often dangerous.

Those who did get an education usually came from better off families in the first place.

Good transport allowed African farmers to export crops like cocoa.

Colonial British rule generally relied on local African leaders. In many ways, traditional societies continued to flourish under colonial rule.

The British built roads, bridges and railways in remote parts of Africa.

British missionaries and officials campaigned strongly to stamp out the slave trade in Africa.

British rule brought improved medical care and education.

Only a small number of Africans benefited from improvements in health and education.

Africans found their own languages, customs and beliefs being pressured by British culture.

For British rule –
supporters of British rule pointed to the benefits it brought

Against British rule –
critics of British rule pointed out that Britain and other European states gained more from colonial rule than the African colonies did

Most African historians generally believe that colonial rule did more for Britain than it did for Africa. It had a more negative effect on Africa than it did on Britain. They would say the scales would tip towards the Against side. Other historians would disagree. A lot depends on how you interpret the evidence. It may seem strange, but the same evidence is often used to try to prove both sides of the argument. It is simply interpreted differently.

Brain work

In pairs or small groups, look at the diagram above showing a set of scales and read the statements in the speech bubbles.

1 Which statements do you think go in which pan?
2 Which way do you think the scales would tip?
3 How far do you think the scales would tip (for example, how many statements on the Against side, how many on the For side)?

The story of South Africa

Today, South Africa's population is a tremendous mix of African, Asian and European people. In a South African city you could meet black Africans who might speak Xhosa, Tswana, Zulu or a wide range of other languages. You could well meet people whose ancestors came from India or China as labourers. You could meet white South Africans whose families originated in Holland, Portugal or Britain. To understand how South Africa has developed like this, you need to look at the different stories that make up South Africa's history.

KEY WORDS

Bantu
Boer
Great Trek
Khoi
Transvaal
Trekboer

Brain work

On pages 156–163 you will read about South Africa from the earliest times to the mid-1800s. Before you start reading, draw up a timeline like the one below.

300 400 500 600 700 800 900 1000 1100 1200 1300 1400 1500 1600 1700 1800 1900

As you read through pages 156–159, note down any important events you come across. You will fill in the rest of your timeline once you have worked through pages 160–163.

The African story: Episode 1

The earliest people in South Africa were bushmen like the Khoi and San peoples. In about AD 300 the Bantu peoples arrived in South Africa. From about 1000 to about 1600 they migrated across most of the eastern half of South Africa, pushing the Khoi into the drier western half. Some Bantu chiefs became powerful from cattle farming and trade and conquered other nations. Source 2 shows the various Bantu peoples in South Africa in around 1600.

The European story: Episode 1

We now turn to what the Europeans were doing in South Africa at this time. Throughout the 1500s the Portuguese, British and Dutch had been sailing past South Africa to trade with India and the rest of Asia.

SOURCE 1 ▼
An enclosed village in the northern part of South Africa, painted in around 1836. Cattle would be kept in the central area at night.

SOURCE 2 ▶

Bantu societies in South Africa in about 1600.

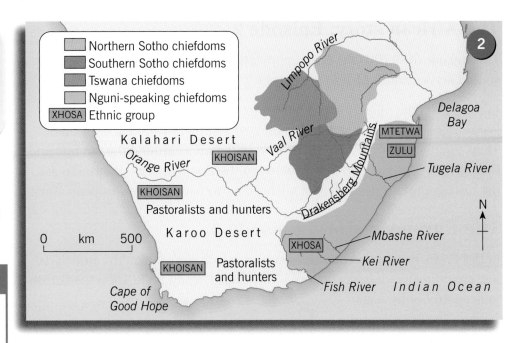

Info point

The Boers

- The Boers were originally Dutch farmers who settled in South Africa and spread across much of its territory.
- They also called themselves Afrikaaners, and spoke their own language – Afrikaans.
- They were tough and independent. They did not like rules or regulations being imposed on them.
- They generally had very large families. Each son wanted a farm as large as his father's. This meant that they needed a lot of land.
- This often caused conflict with other Africans over land.
- The Boers had a religious belief that they were a people chosen by God. They believed that God looked after them.
- They believed that they were superior to the black Africans. They used them as slaves.

SOURCE 3 ▶

An artist's impression of trekboers on the move. The Boers used to put all their possessions into the wagon and bring along slaves and cattle when they moved.

The Cape of Good Hope was a useful stopping-off point for sailors to stock up with supplies. In 1652 the Dutch set up a colony on the Cape (Cape Colony). In 1657 they settled farmers there to raise crops and farm cattle, as well as to trade with the Khoi peoples.

These Dutch farmers or Boers (Boer is the Dutch word for farmer) began to have an impact on South Africa. They soon used up the land around Cape Town and began to spread out. These settler farmers became known as trekboers. They established huge farms of up to 2500 hectares, mostly on land which was also used by the Khoi. The first clashes with the Khoi came in the early 1700s. The Khoi stood little chance. They were scattered and not organised for warfare. The Boers had guns and horses. By the mid 1700s the Khoi had been killed, driven off the land or captured as slaves. By the 1770s the Boers were expanding further into South Africa. They began to move eastwards towards the Orange River and the Fish River. It was not long before there were more clashes with other African peoples.

The African story: Episode 2

Throughout the 1700s the Bantu population increased and Bantu peoples spread across South Africa (see Source 2 on page 157).

In the 1770s the migrating trekboers met with the spreading Bantu. The Bantu were well armed and well organised and there were many of them. They competed with the Boers for land in the areas around the Orange and Fish Rivers. War soon broke out between the Boers and the Bantu. To see the next important development we have to go back to the European story.

The European story: Episode 2

In the 1790s Britain and France went to war with each other. The British did not want the French to get control of the Cape Colony. So in 1806 the British took control of the Cape Colony. The British were only interested in the sea port at the Cape. However, they soon found that they could not ignore what was going on further inland. They were concerned that the Bantu might be a threat to the Cape. As a result, they joined with the Boers against the Bantu. From about 1810 to about 1830, the British concentrated on keeping the Bantu back beyond the Fish River. By that time, other important developments were already taking place.

SOURCE 4 ▼
The importance of South Africa to Britain.

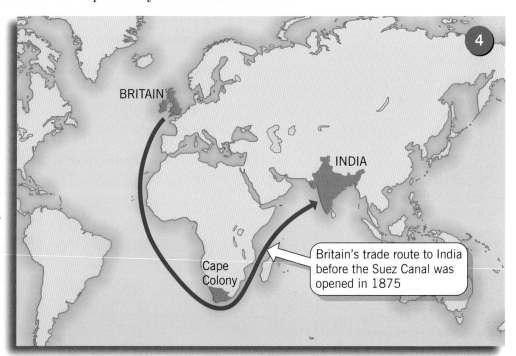

Britain's trade route to India before the Suez Canal was opened in 1875

The African story: Episode 3

In the early 1800s the Bantu people of Africa were suffering. This period became known to Africans as *mfecane*, or 'the crushing'. Drought killed crops and cattle. Some Bantu began to raid others for food and cattle. Raids from Boers and other Europeans made a bad situation even worse. In the midst of this fighting the small Zulu nation emerged as the strongest. The Zulu king, Shaka, was a clever politician and an excellent military leader. In his 12-year rule (1816–1828) the Zulus came to dominate the Bantu peoples, so that they all started to see themselves as Zulus. Soon this mighty new African power would clash with the Europeans.

The European story: Episode 3

At first the Boers accepted being ruled by the British. However, by the 1830s many Boers were unhappy with British rule:

- The British brought about 5000 British settlers to the Cape Colony. The Boers resented these newcomers who were competing for land.
- The British made the Boers pay taxes. This was to pay for the British troops who guarded the frontier against the Bantu Zulus.
- The British banned slavery and gave whites and non-whites the same political rights.

SOURCE 5 ▼
A painting showing Boer farmers on their Great Trek in the 1830s and 1840s. The picture appeared in a book called The Romance of South Africa, *which was published long after the events it was meant to show.*

The African and European story: Episode 4

In 1836–1837 a large number of Boers set out on the Great Trek, a journey to get away from British rule. Over the next ten years some 14,000 Boers emigrated from the Cape Colony. They soon clashed with the Zulus. After a series of running battles they achieved a major victory over the Zulus at Blood River in 1838. They set up their own new Boer colony called Natal. Other Boers set up another Boer state called Transvaal.

Brain work

1 Look at the timeline you created for the Brain work activity on page 156. Fill in any important events about the story of South Africa that you have read on pages 156–159.

2 Look again at pages 156–159. It is important that you understand and remember all the key events on these pages. To make it easier to remember, you are going to give each paragraph in this story a short subheading. The list below has some suggestions, but they are not in the right order. If you can think of better subheadings, use your ideas.

- A mix of peoples • Mfecane and Zulus • Cape Colony
- Boers vs British • Khoi, San and Bantu • Bantu vs Boers
- Trekboers • Great Trek • Europeans arrive • British take Cape Colony

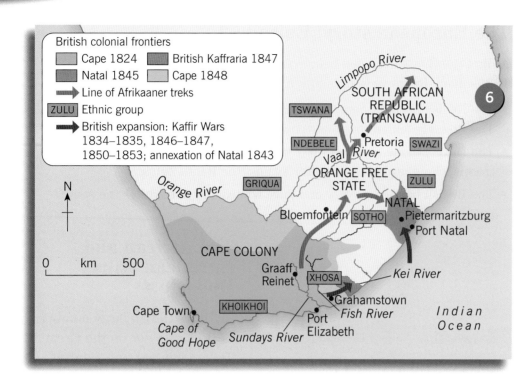

British colonial frontiers
- Cape 1824
- British Kaffraria 1847
- Natal 1845
- Cape 1848
- Line of Afrikaaner treks
- ZULU Ethnic group
- British expansion: Kaffir Wars 1834–1835, 1846–1847, 1850–1853; annexation of Natal 1843

SOUTH AFRICAN REPUBLIC (TRANSVAAL)

TSWANA

NDEBELE   Pretoria   SWAZI

Vaal River

ORANGE FREE STATE   ZULU

Limpopo River

Orange River   GRIQUA

NATAL

Bloemfontein SOTHO   Pietermaritzburg
Port Natal

CAPE COLONY

Graaff Reinet   XHOSA   Kei River

Cape Town

KHOIKHOI

Grahamstown
Fish River
Port Elizabeth

Indian Ocean

Cape of Good Hope   Sundays River

0 km 500

N

KEY WORDS

Uitlander

SOURCE 6 ◀
South Africa in the 1800s.

SOURCE 7 ▼
Soldiers of the 2nd Battalion Natal Native Regiment who fought for the British against the Zulus in the war of 1879.

SOURCE 8 ▶
A cartoon of Cecil Rhodes, published in the 1890s.

SOURCE 9 ▼
Gold mining in the Transvaal, near Johannesburg, 1888.

In the second half of the nineteenth century the British got increasingly drawn in to South Africa's conflicts and troubles:

- In 1843 they took over the Boer colony of Natal. They were concerned that another European state might do this so they got in first.

- In 1867 diamonds were discovered in Griqualand (see Source 6). The Boers and the British both claimed the diamonds. The British took control of the diamond-producing areas.

- In 1877 the British felt that the Boer state of Transvaal was not being governed properly. They took it over. They feared the Zulus would invade it if they did not.

- In 1879 there was a war between the British and the Zulus. After some early Zulu victories, the British effectively destroyed the power of the Zulus.

- In 1881 the Boers rebelled against the British. After some bitter fighting, the British agreed to let the Boers rule the Orange Free State and the Transvaal.

Paul Kruger

- Paul Kruger was the President of the Transvaal. Most Boers looked up to him and admired him as their leader.

- Kruger had travelled on the Great Trek in the 1830s.

- His dream was to unite the four states of South Africa into one Boer state. Gold in the Transvaal gave Kruger the wealth and power which might allow him to achieve that aim.

- He did not trust the British, especially Cecil Rhodes.

- Like most Boers, he believed that they were God's chosen people. He disliked the outsiders (which Boers called Uitlanders) who were flooding into the Transvaal to work the gold mines. He taxed them heavily and did not allow them any political rights (for example, the vote).

Cecil Rhodes

- Cecil Rhodes made his fortune in diamonds in South Africa. He had a reputation for having big ideas and making them work.

- He founded and ran the British South Africa Company. This company was like a small government. He used its resources to take control of lands north of the Transvaal and mine them. These lands later became known as Rhodesia. Local African rulers claimed he had tricked them out of their lands.

- Rhodes built railways to link Rhodesia to the Cape, and dreamed of a Cairo-to-Cape railway to join all Britain's African territories together.

- He became Prime Minister of the Cape Colony in 1890. Like Kruger, he wanted to unite South Africa. But he wanted it to be British.

8

You might think that, after all this conflict, South Africa would then become peaceful. In fact, in the 1880s and 1890s things got worse. The next conflict was triggered when gold was discovered in the Transvaal in 1886. Gold led to the arrival of foreign mining companies, foreign miners (called Uitlanders) and thousands of black African labourers. This soon led to a major clash between the British and the Boers. The story can be told through the aims and actions of two key individuals: Paul Kruger and Cecil Rhodes (see biographies above).

1 How did gold and diamonds affect relations between the Boers and the British?
2 How did gold and diamonds affect the position of black Africans?
3 Look at Source 8. What is the cartoon trying to say about Cecil Rhodes?

Brain work

1 Look at the timeline you created for the Brain work activity on page 156. Fill in any important events you have read about on pages 160–161.

2 Look again at Brain work activity 2 on page 159. Come up with your own headings for the paragraphs on pages 160–161.

Rhodes hoped to stir up trouble between the Boers and the Uitlanders in the Transvaal, and then to move in to 'restore order'. Restoring order really meant taking over. However, his plans were discovered. He was forced to resign in 1896.

This did not help Kruger much. Back in London there was a new British minister in charge of the colonies called Joseph Chamberlain. He also wanted to unite South Africa under British rule. He demanded better treatment for the Uitlanders and the British mining companies. He pushed Kruger so hard that in October 1899 the Boers declared war on the British.

SOURCE 10 ▼
A cartoon from 1896 showing British Colonies Minister Joseph Chamberlain (right) and Boer leader Paul Kruger (left).

A bitter three-year war followed. At first, the Boers had some military successes. However, the enormous resources of the British steadily wore the Boers down. The Boers had about 85,000 soldiers. By the end of the war the British had 450,000 troops in South Africa. They were mostly Indians, but there were also large forces from Canada, New Zealand and Australia. Around 100,000 black Africans were also involved in the war. They were mostly message carriers, scouts and wagon drivers. About 10,000 black Africans fought for the British. African leaders also fought against Boer raiding parties which tried to steal food, cattle and horses.

SOURCE 11 ▼
A Boer farm destroyed by British forces in the Boer War.

In the later stages of the war the Boers stopped fighting in major battles. Instead they adopted hit-and-run tactics. They attacked British patrols, blew up railway lines, and damaged buildings. The British responded by conquering every inch of the Boer lands.

The British destroyed Boer farms. They rounded up Boer families and kept them in concentration camps. Around 28,000 Boers, mostly women and children, died from disease in these camps.

In 1902 the war ended with the Treaty of Vereeniging. South Africa was placed firmly under British control. Many black Africans welcomed the British victory. However, they were soon disappointed. In 1910 South Africa became virtually independent from Britain. The constitution of the new Union of South Africa denied the vote to black South Africans. Other non-white groups also had no say. This was an issue that would continue to torment South Africa until the 1990s.

Brain work

1 Look at the timeline you created for the Brain work activity on page 156. Fill in any important events you have read about the story of South Africa on pages 162–163.

2 Look again at Brain work activity 2 on page 159. Come up with your own headings for the paragraphs on pages 162–163.

3 Why has there been so much conflict in South Africa's history? You need to think about the reasons for conflict.
   a Go through the story of South Africa on pages 156–163 and list all the examples of clashes and conflicts you can find.
   b Summarise the reason for each conflict as briefly as possible.
   c Decide what type of reason it is (for example, competition for land, competition for mineral wealth such as gold or diamonds, competition for political control of South Africa, racial conflict, mixed reasons).
   Use a table like the one below to help you.

Example of clash/conflict	Reason for clash/conflict	Type of clash/conflict

   d Write up your ideas in an essay. You could set it out along these lines.

> There has been conflict in South Africa's history from early times until the early 1900s. There are several reasons for this.
>
> One reason is competition for land. There are many examples of this, such as...
>
> Another reason is competition for mineral wealth (gold, diamonds)...
>
> Competition for political control of South Africa has also caused conflict. For example...
>
> There has also been racial conflict. For instance...
>
> Some conflicts have been the result of different mixed reasons working together at the same time. Examples of this include...
>
> Overall, I feel the main causes of conflict have been...

OVERVIEW

In 1900 Africa was divided into colonies run by various European states. Less than 100 years later Africa was a collection of independent states. In this section you are going to see how this happened, and how one country – South Africa – has coped with the changes of the twentieth century.

SOURCE 1 ▼

The memories of Warhiu Itote. He was a Kenyan who fought in the British army in the Second World War. He then fought against the British to gain independence for Kenya.

6 The first time I ever thought of myself as a Kenyan was in 1943, in the Kalewa trenches on the Burma Front. I'd spent several evenings talking to a British soldier, and thought we had become friends, but I was rather surprised one evening when, after we had been talking for a while, he said, 'You know, sometimes I don't understand you Africans who are out here fighting. What do you think you are fighting for?'

'I'm fighting for the same thing as you are, of course,' I told him.

'I'm not sure that's such a good idea.' I asked him to explain this.

'Look,' he began, 'I'm fighting for England, to preserve my country, my culture, all those things which we Englishmen have built up over the centuries of our history as a nation, including the British Empire. But I can't see why you Africans should fight to protect the Empire instead of fighting to free yourselves. 9

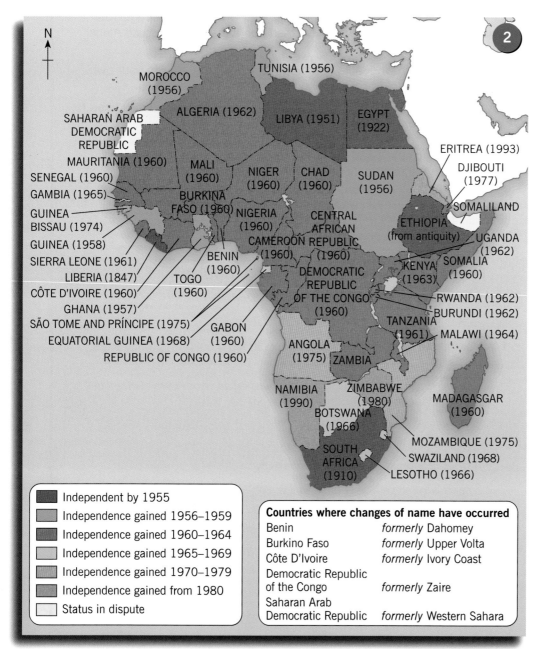

Independent by 1955
Independence gained 1956–1959
Independence gained 1960–1964
Independence gained 1965–1969
Independence gained 1970–1979
Independence gained from 1980
Status in dispute

Countries where changes of name have occurred

Benin	formerly Dahomey
Burkino Faso	formerly Upper Volta
Côte D'Ivoire	formerly Ivory Coast
Democratic Republic of the Congo	formerly Zaire
Saharan Arab Democratic Republic	formerly Western Sahara

SOURCE 2 ◀

A map showing the stages of African independence in the twentieth century.

KEY WORDS

Apartheid
Holocaust
Independence
Nationalism

Independence for Africa

How was independence achieved?

Source 2 shows an independent Africa made up of states which rule themselves. In 1900 most of these states were ruled by European powers. However, by the late 1990s they were all independent, ruled by African peoples. Many factors came together to explain this:

- **The Second World War**: The Second World War changed the history of the world. By 1945 Britain and France were no longer great powers. They did not have the strength or the desire to hold on to their colonies.

- **African nationalism**: Many Africans fought for Britain and France in the Second World War. They met soldiers from the USA, Britain, India and many other African countries. They exchanged political views and ideas. One idea which emerged strongly was that African people should rule themselves. A number of African nationalist leaders emerged who campaigned, persuaded and sometimes fought to gain their country's independence.

- **The Holocaust**: During the Second World War the Nazi leader Adolf Hitler murdered more than six million of Europe's Jews and other minorities because he said they were an inferior race. Ideas about one race being superior to another race were totally discredited. This removed one of the main reasons Europeans gave for ruling African lands and people.

- **Indian independence**: Britain's empire in Asia also began to break up after the Second World War. The most important event was independence for India in 1947. After this, Britain could not really stop any other country becoming independent.

SOURCE 3 ▼

A cartoon published in a British magazine in 1960. The caption was 'The New Africa'.

1 Read Source 1 carefully. Explain how the experience of war led Warhiu Itote to fight for independence for Kenya.

2 Look at Source 3. Explain as fully as you can what the cartoonist is trying to say about the new Africa and how the new Africa has come about. Refer to the information about how independence was achieved to help you.

Has independence helped Africa?

All the countries shown in Source 2 on page 164 are young countries. Some have been relatively successful. For example, Kenya has grown economically, although much of its businesses is owned by foreign companies. Tanzania is poorer than Kenya, but is generally seen as more democratic. There have also been attempts to unite African nations. The most important organisation is called the Organisation for African Unity. This was founded in 1963 to increase cooperation between African states. There have been other organisations with similar aims, such as the Economic Community of West African States. However, African countries have faced many problems since gaining independence:

- There have been civil wars in Congo, Nigeria, Angola and many other states.
- There have been environmental disasters like those in Ethiopia (drought) and Malawi (floods). Often civil war, famine and environmental disaster have come together.

There is no doubt that colonial rule caused many of Africa's problems:

- Many African states found that they were still 'economic colonies'. A good example is Ghana in West Africa. It found that its economy still depended on Britain after it became independent. It still had to sell crops to Britain because it did not have buyers anywhere else in the world.
- Many states found that they were not as independent as they had hoped. European, American and Russian politicians and businesses often interfered in the new states. This led to internal disputes and civil wars.
- Colonial rule left most Africans either badly educated or not educated at all. For example, in East Africa only 1 in 12,000 people received a full secondary education in the 1960s. This meant that there was a shortage of educated people to run government efficiently.
- Other factors have also caused problems and many of these are linked to colonial rule. One of the largest problems is debt. In 1989 over 90 per cent of Africa's production went to pay off interest on debts owed to wealthy countries, mainly in Europe and the USA.

However, African rulers have often caused many of Africa's problems as well (see Sources 5 and 6).

SOURCE 4 ▼

An extract from a speech by Kwame Nkrumah in 1961. Nkrumah was the African nationalist leader who led Ghana to independence from British rule.

❛ For centuries, Europeans dominated the African continent. The white man arrogated [claimed] to himself the right to rule and to be obeyed by the non-white; his mission, he claimed, was to 'civilise' Africa. Under this cloak, the Europeans robbed the continent of vast riches and inflicted unimaginable suffering on the African people.

All this makes a sad story, but now we must be prepared to bury the past with its unpleasant memories and look to the future. All we ask of the former colonial powers is their goodwill and co-operation to remedy past mistakes and injustices and to grant independence to the colonies in Africa. ❜

4

SOURCE 5 ▶

An extract from an article by Tunde Obadina, published in 2000. Tunde Obadina heads a British charity called Africa Business Analysis which publishes articles about African issues.

SOURCE 6 ▶

By Claude Kabemba, an expert on democracy in southern Africa. This extract comes from a radio interview in 2002. He was talking about the problem of food shortages in southern Africa.

SOURCE 7 ▼

A cartoon published in a British newspaper in September 1960. The caption was 'Not for two or three years a clear idea of the future'.

'Blaming all of Africa's problems on colonialism strikes a cord with many educated Africans. [But] simple clear-cut 'them and us' explanations of complex developments are rarely helpful. Focusing on imperialism [colonialisation] has drawn attention away from internal forces which explain some of Africa's problems.

There is no reason why African nations could not have built up their economies so that they did not depend on the rich countries of Europe and the USA. They did not do this because it was not in the interests of the African rulers to do this.'

5

'In this region leaders are more interested in staying in power than they are in serving their people. Governments are more concentrated on politics and they have forgotten social responsibility. Despite the food crisis we are having, most governments are wondering 'How do I access power? How do I stay in power? How do I weaken my opposition?'

They are not wondering about how do we deal with this crisis. Politics has taken over. And that is not good because when we talk about good government, that is the ability of the government to provide services to people. But in many of these countries it's like there is no government, everything is paralysed.'

6

3 Read Source 4.
   a What impact did colonial rule have on Africa?
   b Is the writer bitter about this?

4 Are Sources 4 and 5 written in a similar style?

5 Read Sources 5 and 6.
   a Is the writer saying colonial rule did not harm Africa?
   b What do Sources 5 and 6 agree on?

6 a Look carefully at Source 7 and compare it with Source 3 on page 165. Make a list of all the similarities and differences between the two cartoons.
   b Which of Sources 3 and 7 do you think was the more realistic? Explain your answer.

The story of South Africa (continued)

The story of South Africa continues with the story of the struggle of black South Africans to be treated equally. The end of this story comes in 1994. Nelson Mandela spent his whole life fighting for the rights of black people in South Africa. He spent most of his life in prison. Yet in 1994 he was able to vote in South Africa's first democratic elections (see Source 1). He also went on to win those elections and become South Africa's president.

Apartheid

As you saw on page 163, South Africa became independent from Britain in 1910. At this time, only white South Africans had full rights. This division became even more severe in 1948. The government brought in a series of laws which became known as apartheid. Here are just a few of the restrictions that apartheid placed on non-white South Africans. This is what apartheid meant in practice:

- Every South African was classified by race. Identity cards and pass laws meant that non-whites were not free to move around in their own country.
- In the towns, black South Africans had to live in separate areas away from the white population. They were allowed to travel into the towns to work.
- In the countryside, black South Africans were forced to live in homelands called Bantustan. These were generally overcrowded, unhealthy and poor.
- Everyday facilities such as shops, toilets, public transport, beaches, hospitals and ambulances were segregated, which means blacks were not allowed to use the same facilities as non-blacks.
- Sex and marriage between the races became illegal.
- In 1956 the black Africans who did have the vote had this privilege taken away from them.

SOURCE 3 ▶

Extracts from the United Nations (UN) Universal Declaration of Human Rights, 1948. The UN was set up in 1945 as a place for the countries of the world to sort out disputes and work together to make the world a better place.

SOURCE 1 ◀

Nelson Mandela casting his vote in the 1994 South African elections.

SOURCE 2 ◀

Apartheid signs in South Africa in the 1950s.

❛ **You have the same human rights as everyone else in the world, because you are a human being. These rights cannot be taken away from you. Everybody, no matter who they are or where they live, should be treated with dignity.**　③

You should not be treated differently, nor have your rights taken away, because of your race, colour, sex, language, religion or political opinions.

Everyone has the right to:
- **life, liberty and security.**
- **freedom from slavery and servitude.**
- **be treated as a person in the eyes of the law and to a fair trial.**
- **move about freely within your country, and to travel to and from your own country and to leave any country.**
- **marry, regardless of their race, country or religion.**
- **own property.**
- **freedom of opinion and expression.**
- **take part in government.**
- **equal pay for equal work.**
- **education.** ❜

Fighting apartheid

From the early 1900s black South Africans resisted the restrictions on them. In 1912 the Native National Congress was formed, which protested against the restrictions. It later became the African National Congress (ANC). By the 1930s this organisation represented black, mixed race and Asian South Africans as well.

The response of the ANC to apartheid was a campaign of protest and civil disobedience. A common protest was burning pass books. Black South Africans had to carry a pass at all times. This pass showed where and when they were allowed to travel. The government responded to peaceful protests with beatings, arrests and further harsh laws. By 1960 most of the ANC leaders were in jail and the ANC itself was declared illegal.

1 In pairs or small groups, discuss how the South African apartheid regime compares to the UN's Declaration of Human Rights.

2 Write your own definition of apartheid for a 'Dictionary of Historical Terms'.

3 Write a definition of the ANC for the dictionary.

The arrests did not stop the protests, and matters came to a head with the Sharpeville Massacre of 1961. On 21 March 1961 peaceful protesters were shot at by the Sharpeville police and 69 were killed. Strikes and protests broke out and condemnation flooded in from all over the world. The UN Security Council officially condemned the South African regime for the first time.

The ANC turns to violence

In response to Sharpeville, the ANC began a campaign of violence. This was not very successful. Many ANC leaders were arrested, including Nelson Mandela in 1962. Other ANC fighters fled South Africa and went into training camps in the countries which bordered it.

At the same time, other protests continued. In the 1970s a new generation of protesters wrote books, sang songs and published pamphlets about the evils of apartheid. The movement was known as Black Consciousness. School students played a key role in Black Consciousness. In June 1976 over 500 demonstrators were shot dead in the township of Soweto, most of them schoolchildren. Soweto erupted into protests and riots that lasted for months.

Apartheid begins to crumble

In many ways, Soweto was a turning point. The world was outraged. The governments in America and Europe began to cut off business links between South Africa and the outside world. Even more seriously, the oil-producing countries of Arabia cut off oil supplies to South Africa. Finally, there was internal pressure from inside South Africa. The ANC was gaining so much support that businesses were afraid that there would be a revolution.

SOURCE 4 ▲
Some of the victims of the Sharpeville Massacre.

SOURCE 5 ▼
A cartoon from a British newspaper published in January 1990.

"OBVIOUSLY WE CAN'T LEAVE HIM IN HERE MUCH LONGER."

> **❝** I challenge the right of the Court to hear my case on two grounds. Firstly I challenge it because I fear that I will not be given a fair and proper trial. Second, I consider myself neither legally nor morally bound to obey laws made by a parliament in which I have no representation. In a political trial such as this one, which involves a clash of the aspirations of the African people and those of whites, the country's courts, as presently constituted, cannot be impartial and fair. The white man makes all the laws, he drags us before his courts and accuses us, and he sits in judgement over us. **❞**

(6)

SOURCE 6 ▲
An extract from a speech made by Nelson Mandela at his trial in 1964.

SOURCE 7 ▶
Mandela speaking on the Bantu Education Bill 1953.

Nelson Mandela

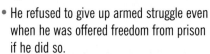

- Nelson Mandela was born in 1918.
- He formed the ANC Youth League with Oliver Tambo in 1944.
- He contributed to the ANC Programme of Action in 1949.
- He qualified in law and practised in Johannesburg until 1952.
- Mandela became a member of the executive of the ANC in 1952.
- He travelled across South Africa in the 1950s.
- He took part in the 1959 Pass Book demonstrations.
- After an eight-month trial, he was sentenced to life imprisonment in 1964.
- Mandela continued to be the leading figure in the ANC.
- He refused to give up armed struggle even when he was offered freedom from prison if he did so.
- He was released from prison in 1990.
- Mandela became President of South Africa in May 1994.

By 1989 it was clear that a new approach was needed. The man given the job was President F W de Klerk. De Klerk removed the ban which made the ANC and other black nationalist groups illegal in February 1990. Within months the key figure of the ANC, Nelson Mandela, was freed after 27 years in jail. Mandela and the ANC began to hold talks with the government. More violence and arguments followed, but in September 1992 de Klerk and Mandela finally agreed on the way forward. In April 1994 South Africa held its first free elections and Nelson Mandela became President of South Africa in May of that year.

> **❝** The aim of this law is to teach our children that Africans are inferior to Europeans. You must defend the right of the African parents to decide the kind of education that shall be given to their children. Teach the children that Africans are not one iota inferior to Europeans. **❞**

(7)

Brain work

Imagine that Nelson Mandela is coming to your school to open a new building. You have been chosen to introduce him to the whole school before he gives a short speech to the students.

Prepare a three-minute talk to introduce Nelson Mandela. You should mention some of the following things:

- Basic information like where he comes from and the jobs he has done.
- His main beliefs.
- Why he is an important person.
- His contribution to the history of South Africa.
- Your own personal views on Nelson Mandela and his achievements.

Why does African history cause so many arguments?

KEY WORDS
Propaganda

In this unit you have come across many controversial events, ideas and opinions. African history has generated many controversies (see Sources 1 and 2).

> " Africa is not a part of the world's history. There have been no important historical movements or developments in Africa. African peoples have not developed true societies or civilisations. They must be led to civilisation by other peoples, that is, by the peoples of Europe, and most particularly of Britain and France. **"** ①

> " Perhaps in the future there will be some African history to teach. But at present there is none or very little. There is only the history of the Europeans in Africa [from about 1600]. **"** ②

SOURCE 1 ◀
An extract from the Philosophy of History *written by the European writer Georg Hegel in the late 1820s.*

SOURCE 2 ◀
A British historian writing in 1966 in a book called The Rise of Christian Europe. *(You have come across this source already on page 141.)*

1 Read Source 1. If it did not have a date on it, would you have guessed it was from the 1800s? Explain your answer.

2 Read Source 2. Does the writer in 1966 agree completely with the writer in the 1820s?

3 Explain how you might feel if someone said that Britain had no history.

4 Explain what evidence you could use to argue against the views in Sources 1 and 2.

Views like Source 1 were still widely held until the 1960s. For example, look at Source 2. When this was written, it caused outrage among African people and historians who specialised in African history.

In one way, this was a good thing: it helped to spur on African historians. If you search for African history on the Internet today, you will find thousands of websites on the subject. You can also buy hundreds of books on all kinds of topics about African history.

Of course, this does not mean that nobody argues about African history any more. For example, in 1989 an American writer called Kevin Shillington published a book called 'A History of Africa'. Sources 3 and 4 show that there were very different reactions to this book.

SOURCE 3 ▶

Comments by African historians on Kevin Shillington's book A History of Africa.

> 'Shillington's coverage is comprehensive, his presentation clear, and his content well up to date with the latest research...'
> *J B Peires, University of Transkei*
>
> '...a work with many virtues... stylistic lucidity, profusion of clear maps and excellent illustrations.'
> *International Journal of African Historical Studies*

SOURCE 4 ▶

A selection of reviews of Kevin Shillington's book. They were written between 1995 and 2001 by American readers.

> • *Review 1*: Historically inaccurate and biased. I am a fan of Shillington and I expected more from this book. His effort to glorify African leaders and condemn Europeans makes this text biased and inaccurate.
> • *Review 2*: The worst Africa survey I have yet encountered. The book is nothing more than pro-African propaganda. It is not thought-provoking, as all of Africa's ills are blamed on Western colonialism. It's aimed at a high-school or lower audience. It seems Shillington is more concerned with increasing the damaged self-esteem of black students than with providing an accurate history that will allow those students to see the world realistically.
> • *Review 3*: Absolutely outstanding for survey courses! The book does not get bogged down into too much detail but has the most important concepts, people and events. We use it at the Air Force Academy every year with no plans to change in the near future.

5 Describe the reaction of the readers in Source 3 to this book.
6 Read Source 4.
a Make a list of all the points the reviewers liked about the book.
b Make a list of all the points the reviewers did not like.

So, you can see that it is not easy to write about African history! Look back over this section and decide how you think we have done.

Key words

abbey	large church and connected buildings run by monks (same as a monastery). *p. 70*
abbot	chief monk in an abbey. *p. 70*
AD	dates which come after the birth of Jesus Christ. *p. 5*
administration	running of the government, e.g. law and order, taxes. *p. 18*
adviser	official who helped the emperor or monarch make decisions. *pp. 36, 54*
African National Congress (ANC)	organisation which opposed apartheid in South Africa. *p. 168*
ambassador	official who represents a ruler. *p. 126*
Americas	term used to describe North and South America. *p. 142*
amphitheatre	stadium where games took place. *p. 6*
apartheid	political system which separated white and non-white South Africans. *p. 165*
aqueduct	structure for carrying water. *p. 6*
Arabia	Roman province in what is today the Middle East. Area between the Red Sea and the Persian Gulf. *pp. 18, 122*
archaeological	evidence from pottery, bones and other materials found underground. *pp. 6, 90, 116*
archaeologist	scientist who tries to understand the past by studying the remains of old buildings, objects, bodies, etc. *pp. 18, 116*
archbishop	very important priest in the Christian Church, e.g. Archbishop Becket was in charge of the Christian Church in England. *p. 60*
archer	soldier who uses a bow and arrow *pp. 18, 54*
Asia Minor	modern-day Turkey. *p. 34*
auxiliary	Roman soldier with specialist skills, e.g. archer, horse soldier. *p. 18*
Bantu	one group of African peoples. *p. 156*
barbarian	someone who lived outside the Roman Empire. *p. 5*
baron	important figure who usually owned a lot of land and controlled many knights. *p. 54*
BC	dates which come before the birth of Jesus Christ. *p. 5*
benefactor	person who helps someone, usually with a gift. *p. 18*
bestiarii	type of gladiator. *p. 36*
Bible	holy book sacred to Jews (Old Testament) and Christians (Old and New Testament). *p. 122*
bishop	senior figure in the Christian Church. *pp. 50, 54*
Boer	white South Africans descended from Dutch settlers. *p. 156*
brand	using a red-hot iron to make a mark on a slave. *p. 30*
British Empire	territories ruled by Britain. *p. 150*
brooch	type of jewellery, like a modern badge but used to hold on clothing like togas or cloaks. *p. 34*
burgess	merchant or businessman working in towns. *p. 65*
burial	putting the dead to rest in the ground or in a tomb. *p. 34*
bushel	measure of wheat. *p. 90*
bustum	special type of burial involving a funeral fire. *p. 34*
Byzantine Empire	the eastern half of the old Roman Empire which continued until the 1400s. *p. 122*
caliph	Muslim ruler. *p. 122*
campaign	war or series of battles. *pp. 18, 110, 142*
campaigning	fighting. *p. 68*
carding	straightening out wool fibres to get them ready for spinning. *p. 90*
Carthage	city in North Africa which fought several wars with Rome. *p. 12*
cathedral	very large and beautiful church. *p. 65*
cavalry	soldiers on horseback. *pp. 18, 54*
centurion	officer in the Roman army. *p. 28*
charter	important legal document. *p. 80*
Christendom	lands where the Christians lived. *p. 70*
Christian	someone who follows the teachings of Jesus Christ. *pp. 5, 122*
Christianity	the religion based on the teachings of Jesus Christ. *pp. 6, 122*
citizen	person who had full rights in Ancient Rome. *p. 5*
citizenship	being a citizen of the Roman Empire, which gave special privileges. *p. 28*
civilisation	people living together with a government, and usually with towns and cities. *p. 116*
civil rights	rights which allow people to play a full role in society, e.g. to vote. *p. 5*
civil war	war between people from the same country, empire, city. *p. 5*
clergymen	general term for all priests. *p. 76*
cleric	name for all types of priests. *p. 70*
colonial	relating to colonies – lands ruled by other countries. *p. 132*
colonialism	process of taking over other countries and ruling them as colonies. *p. 152*
colony	territory ruled by another country. *p. 152*
Colosseum	the main stadium in Rome. *p. 36*

conquer	taking over another country or people. pp. 5, 54, 116
conquest	taking over another country or people. pp. 5, 116
continent	large area of land. p. 114
count	important landowner, similar to a baron. p. 60
critic	an opponent. p. 152
crusading	going on crusade to defeat the Muslims who had taken over the Holy Land. p. 68
Dacia	Roman province; modern-day Romania. p. 18
demesne	land owned by the lord of the village. p. 86
depopulation	when people leave an area. p. 150
deposed	forced to give up power. p. 47
duke	important ruler of a territory (e.g. Normandy) – almost as important as a king. p. 54
dyeing	using colours (dye) to colour cloth. p. 102
dynasty	a family of rulers passing the throne from one to the next. p. 116
earl	important and powerful landowner in England. p. 54
election	selecting a government by voting for them. p. 168
emperor	ruler of an empire. p. 5
empire	a state made up of several countries or territories ruled by one ruler (emperor). pp. 5, 114
enclosed	fenced off. p. 90
Etruscans	people who ruled the area around Rome before the Romans. p. 5
excommunicate	to throw out of the Christian Church. p. 80
finances	money. p. 110
fine	punishment for breaking a law (to pay a fine). p. 80
flogged	beaten with a whip or stick. p. 76
fortifications	strong walls or ditches to protect a territory. p. 48
fortress	castle or strong, secure building. pp. 76, 137
Forum	central area of Roman cities. p. 6
freedman	slave who had gained freedom. p. 24
frontier	border between the empire and the lands outside. p. 28
Gaul	area of the Roman Empire where France is today. p. 5
gladiator	fighter in Roman games. p. 34
Goths	people from northern Europe who invaded the Roman Empire and settled in North Africa in the 400s. pp. 47, 126
government	people who run states, countries or empires by making laws, organising armies, collecting taxes, etc. pp. 6, 54, 116
governor	official who ran a province of the Roman Empire; person who rules over a particular area. pp. 18, 132
Great Trek	journey made by Boers in the early 1800s. p. 156
Greeks	people from Greece who settled over a wide area, including southern Italy. p. 11
griot	poet whose job was to remember the history of important African families. p. 132
guardian	man who stood in the place of a father. p. 42
harmony	living together in peace. p. 18
harvest	bringing in the crops when they are fully grown. p. 90
hierarchy	society with rich people at the top and the majority at the bottom with less wealth and power. p. 116
hieroglyphics	Egyptian form of writing. p. 116
historian	person who researches and writes about past events. pp. 11, 54, 116
Holocaust	murder of millions of Jews and other races by the Nazis in the Second World War. p. 165
Holy Land	the area where Jesus Christ lived and died; modern-day Palestine/Israel. p. 68
Huns	people from central Asia who invaded the Roman Empire in the 400s. p. 47
incense	sweet-smelling smoke. p. 34
independence	African states ruling themselves and becoming independent from the European states which had ruled them. p. 165
inferior	not very good. p. 114
inherit	to take over the wealth or property of parents or other family members. p. 80
Islam	religion of Muslims. p. 122
Jesus	the son of God, in Christian beliefs. pp. 76, 122
Jew	person from Judea – modern-day Israel. pp. 30, 70, 122
Judaism	the religion of Jews. p. 122
judge	official who decided what happened in legal disputes. p. 28
Khoi	group of African people who lived in south and central Africa. p. 156
knight	soldier who fights for a baron or earl in return for lands or similar types of payment. p. 54
Lancastrian	belonging to the Lancaster family. p. 110
Latin	language of the Romans. p. 6

Latins	the tribe that originally lived around Rome and eventually became the Romans. *p. 11*
legacy	what a person or people leave behind them, e.g. ideas, buildings, religion. *p. 116*
legal	allowed by law. *p. 65*
legion	the Roman army was made up of legions of about 5000 men. *p. 12*
legionary	Roman soldier. *p. 19*
loathsome	unpleasant. *p. 142*
locust	type of insect. *p. 118*
lord	an important landowner who could be a knight, earl or duke. *p. 54*
malaria	deadly sickness spread by mosquitoes. *p. 50*
mason	stone worker. *p. 137*
medieval	period running from about AD 700 to about AD 1500. *p. 54*
merchant	trader. *pp. 19, 65*
Mesopotamia	lands to the east of the Roman Empire; modern-day Iraq. *p. 19*
migrating	moving to another home. *p. 47*
military	relating to war. *pp. 15, 126*
minister	another name for a priest. *p. 70*
Mithras	god worshipped by Persians and also by many Romans. *p. 24*
monarch	king or queen. *p. 54*
monastery	large church and connected buildings run by monks (same as an abbey). *p. 70*
monk	man who gave up his life to serve God, usually belonging to an order of monks and living in a monastery away from the outside world. *p. 56*
monument	statue, building or similar object built to help people remember someone. *p. 80*
mortar	cement that holds bricks together. *p. 137*
mosaic	decorated tiles used on walls and floors. *p. 6*
mosque	Muslim place of worship. *p. 126*
Muhammad	the chief prophet of the Muslim faith. *p. 122*
murmillone	type of gladiator. *p. 36*
Muslim	follower of Islam. *p. 122*
mythical	coming from ancient stories. *p. 36*
nationalism	wanting to be a nation. *p. 165*
naval	relating to the sea. *p. 12*
New Testament	second part of the Bible, sacred to Christians. *p. 122*
Norman Conquest	successful takeover of England by Normans in 1066. *p. 54*
Normandy	area of modern France which was ruled by the Duke of Normandy from the 900s onwards. *p. 54*
nun	woman who gave up her life to serve God (like a monk). *p. 70*
official	person who helped to run the government, usually a priest or monk. *p. 54*
Old Testament	first part of the Bible, sacred to Christians and Jews. *p. 122*
overthrow	collapse. *p. 53*
parson	local priest in the village. *p. 86*
paterfamilias	father of the family, usually the oldest male in the house. *p. 42*
patronising	treating someone as though they are simple. *p. 152*
Pax Romana	Roman Peace; the order kept by the Roman Empire at its height. *p. 24*
peasant	typical farm worker; majority of population in medieval England (also known as villein). *p. 54*
persecute	to attack someone because of their beliefs. *p. 50*
Persia	area to the east of the Roman Empire; modern-day Iran. *p. 24*
petty burgess	owner of a small business, e.g. a shopkeeper. *p. 65*
pharaoh	Egyptian ruler. *p. 118*
pilgrim	person who travelled to a holy place to praise God. *p. 70*
pilgrimage	journey to a holy place. *pp. 70, 122*
plague	deadly disease, also called the Black Death. *pp. 50, 90*
plantation	large-scale farm. *p. 145*
Pope	head of the Roman Catholic Church. *p. 70*
Portuguese	people from Portugal. *p. 137*
priestess	female priest who was thought to be a link between humans and the gods. *p. 36*
prisoner of war	enemy soldier captured in battle, usually made into a slave. *p. 36*
propaganda	method of spreading ideas or information. *p. 172*
prophet	person who has heard the word of God. *p. 122*
province	area which made up a section of the Roman Empire, e.g. Britain was a province. *p. 19*
psalter	prayer book. *p. 90*
Qur'an	Holy book of the Islamic faith. *p. 122*